Boomer Girls

Boomer

Girls

Poems by Women from the Baby Boom Generation

Edited by **Pamela Gemin** & **Paula Sergi**

UNIVERSITY OF IOWA PRESS IOWA CITY

University of Iowa Press, Iowa City 52242

Printed in the United States of America
Design by Richard Hendel
http://www.uiowa.edu/~uipress

Printed on acid-free paper
Library of Congress Cataloging-in-Publication Data
Boomer girls: poems by women from the baby boom generation / edited by Pamela Gemin and Paula Sergi.
p. cm.
ISBN 0-87745-698-4, ISBN 0-87745-687-9 (pbk.)
1. American poetry—Women authors. 2. Women—United States poetry. 3. Baby boom generation poetry. 4. American poetry—20th century. I. Gemin, Pamela, 1954– . II. Sergi, Paula, 1952– .
PS589.B66 1999
811′.540809287—dc21 99-14972

99 00 01 02 03 C 5 4 3 2 1

99 00 01 02 03 P 5 4 3 2

To my Boomer girlfriends and to

Boomer Girls everywhere—to us!

P. G.

To my sisters Nina and Laura, Boomers both,

and to the girlfriends I've grown up with—you know

who you are.

P. S.

Contents

Introduction

When *Life* celebrates our generation's coming of age with a special issue; when Barbie turns 40 and finds herself worthy of serious cultural study; when every other catalog in the mailbox tempts us with glossy visions of lava lamps, Gumbys, and bubble-tire bikes; when we open the latest fashion magazines and see that the teased-up flips, poker-straight bangs, and frosted lipsticks we wore in high school are back, along with our satin shirts, glittery nails and—God forbid—even our three-level platform shoes; we know what's gone around has indeed come around, and we've finally come of age in the U.S.A. And American women Baby Boomers, the Boomer Girls whose mothers may have toiled with wringer washers and ironed pillowcases sprinkled with water from Coke bottles, and whose daughters may be writing graduate theses on laptop computers and e-mailing from Brazil, have ridden the wildest wave of change to rip through their culture since the women's suffrage movement: the Second Wave of Feminism.

Where were you between Betty Crocker and Gloria Steinem? was the question that began our call for submissions to *Boomer Girls*, an anthology of coming-of-age poems by women born between 1945 and 1964, give or take a few years on either side. The answers came in a steady stream of more than 300 submissions, from November 1996 to May 1997, in crisp white #10 envelopes, official-looking manila clasp envelopes, or padded mailing bags too full to seal properly, their poems spilling out like urgent messages. On Friday nights, sprawled out on Pam's living room floor with glasses of wine, or Saturday mornings, sitting in Paula's kitchen with coffee and bagels, we read them to each other, despite interruptions from four cats (who recklessly dove into piles of poems and sent the pages flying), two children, two husbands, five hundred students, telephones, doorbells, oven timers, buzzing dryers. . . . Some poems, like Barbara Crooker's "Nearing Menopause, I Run into Elvis at Shoprite" made us laugh out loud; others, like Alison Townsend's "Supplies," put tears on our eyes. Each poem gave us yet another piece of the big picture, a portrait of our generation of women painted in their various colors, creeds, and classes on the wide-open canvas of common experience.

Boomer Girls takes our generation's women from birth through childhood, adolescence, and young womanhood into motherhood and on to middle age, where we reflect upon who we are, what we've become, what we're still becoming, and how we've come to define ourselves as Americans. In *Where the Girls Are,* Susan J. Douglas describes the unique cultural history that Boomer Girls share, united "by Walt Disney, the nightly news, Mark Eden bust developers, *The Mary Tyler Moore Show*, Cyndi Lauper, and ads for skin creams with 'advanced delivery systems' and . . . internalizing an endless film loop of fairy-tale princesses, beach bunnies, witches, flying nuns, bionic women, and beauty queens, a series of flickering images that urged us, since childhood, to be all these things all the time [and] to know which persona to assume when" (18).

These contradictory images surface not only in advertising and pop culture media, however, but also in more serious endeavors by women artists. A new generation of women poets, whose craft requires them to synthesize large issues using the fewest possible words, or celebrate the small wonders of daily life by awarding them the larger consideration they deserve, has taken up the task of recording and reflecting upon the enormous changes their lives have witnessed, collectively and individually, since the beginning of their cultural awareness.

Poets like Lucille Clifton, Carolyn Kizer, Alicia Ostriker, Marge Piercy, and Adrienne Rich broke ground for *Boomer Girls*' poets, who now begin to take their rightful places beside them. "When I read [this new generation's] poems," says Eavan Boland in her introduction to Harriet Levin's *The Christmas Show*, "I see that they tried out their first lipsticks, had their first sexual experiences, wrote their first poems against a backdrop of space exploration, in the aftermath of the Vietnam war, to the noise of household gods falling, . . . they had read Plath, Bishop, and Rich by the time they knew they were poets. Their poems avail easily of the lyric and narrative distinctions which have been so much a part of the vocabulary of American poetry since the Second World War" (xiii).

So who are the Boomer Girls? They are daughters named for abolitionists or storybook heroines, dressed up as angels or geisha girls or dressing their own paper dolls, as they do in Geraldine Connolly's poem "Movie Queens," "in shimmering lilts of cloth / and color, / foxfur stoles, / ornaments of pearl and sequin." They are girls playing sick and nursing other girls, girls watching *Queen for a Day*, "bathed / in the blue TV light, / trying to be good," as Dorianne Laux describes them in "Small Gods." Or perhaps they are fighting each other on playgrounds, belly-flopping off docks, running through fire hydrant sprays, sleeping in tents, or staying up all night at slumber parties. They are girls finding faith in radio songs, posing as grown-up women in vanity mirrors, hula-hooping, hulling strawberries, watching men land on the moon. And always, there is music playing—in the kitchen, in the car, on the transistor—the Four Tops, Marvin Gaye, the Temptin' Temps, Janis Joplin, Patsy Cline, Johnny Cash, Sam Cooke, the Rolling Stones, the Ronettes, Van Morrison, Otis Redding. . . .

The Boomer Girls are Italian, Portuguese, African American, Irish, German, Latina, Finn, Native American, and rich blends of all of the above and more, praying in Sunday service or pregnant in the garden of a home for girls, listening for "the vibration of pistil and stamen," as in Heid Erdrich's "Creation." They are Catholic, Jewish, Protestant, Buddhist, Mennonite. Like Kathryn Daniels's persona in "Big Sister Says, 1967," they learn that "beauty hurts," learn to bake cookies, learn to slow dance with boys at basement parties. They spend hours locked in bathrooms; they consult *Peyton Place* or search dictionaries for "the real words" for what Julia Alvarez calls their "heart's desire," their "body's breaking." They smoke their first cigarettes, take their first drinks. They skip evening rosary to shop at the mall, make out with boys in parked cars, scoop ice cream for summer tourists. They write their first poems.

Soon enough they find strength in numbers, as they do in Leslie Adrienne Miller's poem "Lawn Ornaments," in which a gang of seven high-school girls piles into "someone's father's finned Buick" and drives into the night, "in the charged air / of female rage" to seek revenge on an indifferent boy, "armed / with laughter." And sometimes they suffer—they drink too much, eat too little, waste their love on the wrong partners. Ultimately, they find peace and solidarity in friendships, faith in themselves, hope in the faces of their children. They begin to cherish their mothers' and fathers' stories, explore and reclaim their heritage. They grow into their names, as in Harriet Jacobs's poem to Harriet Tubman: "the sound . . . steady as my own breath." As they grow older, they reexamine their lives, claim their places in the grand scheme that has suddenly become their world, their children's inheritance. They struggle with the demands of adulthood, the price of responsibility, the ever-evolving issues of politics, gender, sexuality, self-image, and race, as Elizabeth Alexander does in "Affirmative Action Blues (1993)": "Right now two black people sit in a jury room / in Southern California trying to persuade / nine white people that what they saw when four white / police officers brought batons back like / they were smashing a beautiful piñata was / 'a violation of Rodney King's civil rights.'" As they face parenthood, divorce, infertility, and the issues of middle age, they contemplate the "second half" of their lives, as Joyce Sutphen does in "Crossroads": "There will be new dreams every night, / and the drapes will never be closed. / I will toss my string of keys into a deep / well and old letters into the grate." Finally, they "Let Go," in Dianne Seuss-Brakeman's rollicking celebration of women's lives and "release the old thunder, the old unspoken storms." Who are the Boomer Girls? We could never include them all. But their colorful stories are woven in and around and between the lines of these poems, delivered in the voices of daughters, mothers, lovers, poet laureates, angels, and waitresses—all of them revolutionaries.

ACKNOWLEDGMENTS

We would like to thank Sandra Ahrens, Karen Austin, Marguerite Helmers, David Graham, Julie King, Estella Lauter and the University of Wisconsin Oshkosh English Department, John Reinhard, Maureen Seaton, Marian Sheridan, Kate Sontag, Deb Zwicky, and the staff at the Fond du Lac Arts Center for their energetic support throughout this project. Special thanks to our families: Patricia and William Pierce and Joseph Gemin; Evelyn Wettstein and Michael, Greg, and Frank Sergi. Sincere gratitude also to Holly (Onward!) Carver, our editor at the University of Iowa Press, who paved the way.

1
The Small Knowledge of Our Bodies

SANDRA CISNEROS

My Wicked Wicked Ways

This is my father.
See? He is young.
He looks like Errol Flynn.
He is wearing a hat
that tips over one eye,
a suit that fits him good,
and baggy pants.
He is also wearing
those awful shoes,
the two-toned ones
my mother hates.

Here is my mother.
She is not crying.
She cannot look into the lens
because the sun is bright.
The woman,
the one my father knows,
is not here.
She does not come till later.

My mother will get very mad.
Her face will turn red
and she will throw one shoe.
My father will say nothing.
After a while everyone
will forget it.
Years and years will pass.
My mother will stop mentioning it.

This is me she is carrying.
I am a baby.
She does not know
I will turn out bad.

DIANE SEUSS-BRAKEMAN

What Is There

What is there to remember?
Spilled milk, milky-skinned dad,
Hazy mom in a yellow blouse
And a crib full of decals—a container.
Later the kid stubs her toe, runs
Away. The feelings were flat
As flatware, weren't they? Or was
She dark and deep, curly-haired
And lonely? Was the loneliness
A cake? Deep brown and damp
With chocolate? Did she cry
With regret, sucking her fingers
Until the cows came home? Was
Her small body tender as a tree-toad's,
Quiet-chested and birdbath-still?
Or was she like the wasps that
Beat the screen door senseless
All summer, hard-assed
And full of poison?

JAN BEATTY

If This Is Sex, It Must Be Tuesday

So it was every week on a Tuesday,
that you and your friend, Ginny,
strayed from the dance at St. Anselm's
to Duquesne Gardens, feigning interest
in hockey, waiting to get laid.
I can picture it—you in fake cashmere
with pearl buttons, a gabardine skirt
that hit you at midcalf, you and Ginny
shuffling popcorn till last period,
when you'd freshen your lips with TORRID RED
for the after game party at the Webster Hall dorms.
After all, these were the Pittsburgh Hornets,
this was 1951, and you were a poor Irish girl
from Garfield with a hard drive for excitement,
and hockey was it, getting cross-checked by the best,
having stories to tell in your lean, checkered life,
left with no father, a reluctant sister,
and a mother who cleaned houses for the rich.
So when did I happen, this one-night stand
with the MVP after his big, icy win,
the second Tuesday in February, or the third?
Do you remember the feel of his hands on you?
Were they rough, or tender, were they bloody
from fighting? And when your belly grew into
the body you never wanted, did you curse me,
try to cut me? Should I say you did your best,
a spare girl from a broken family,
or should I say it straight—
you wanted it, you took it, like we all do,
you lied to save yourself, you gave away
part of your heart, you couldn't
wish it right.

PAULA GOLDMAN

Atlantic City Snapshot, 1944

Eight ladies walk arm in arm
uniformly jeweled and coiffured
under a billboard of a
Coppertone baby
above the boardwalk.
I am not born yet.

Mother wears a Persian lamb
coat, shoulder bag and black-beaded
beret. Her dark-gloved hand holds
the thin strap in place,
a hand that will not
soothe my tearful face.

Such a sad face mother makes,
the gray photograph torn above
her head as if forked lightning
had struck her forlorn
on this bright day. She
never liked herself

in pictures. Shadows fall,
point to noon at Kentucky Ave.
and the boardwalk. I will buy
and sell properties
in Monopoly
over and over,

and lose to avaricious
brothers, but never will I part
with this dressup version of
Mother who wore blood-
stained aprons in a
kosher meat market.

Mother, who stunk of sweat, wears
black open-toed shoes, a dash
of Arpège, and her regrets
for the camera.
I smell the photo
for the ocean's salt

spray, but it's a different
ocean. I have not taken in
my first wave or plunged into
the hot sand, trembling
from the cold, my first
home, the Atlantic.

The boardwalk is the home of
the original saltwater
taffy—Fralinger's. I try
to smell the candy
stores lining the boards
under the hotels

where Mother's walking. Hotels
built like sand castles span a time
before and after I am
born when Father goes
to jail for having
sold meat on the black

market, his name—*our name*—spread
on the front page of the A.C.
paper. No wonder Mother's
lips are pressed tightly
and her eyes look out at the camera

hopelessly, but it took years
to find out—it wasn't my fault,
the sadness, I mean, and not
even my father's
business. It's before
I'm in the picture.

Naming

born at the end
of the Second World War

I was not named
for a great-aunt in Russia

or a grandmother
baking challah in Brooklyn

but for Peter Pan's
Wendy Darling

who flew away
to Neverland

by thinking only lovely
wonderful thoughts

True Myth

Tell a child she is composed of parts
(her Ojibway quarters, her German half-heart)
she'll find the existence of harpies easy
to swallow. Storybook children never come close
to her mix, but manticores make great uncles,
Sphinx a cousin she'll allow, centaurs better to love
than boys—the horse part, at least, she can ride.
With a bestiary for a family album she's proud.
Her heap of blankets, her garbage grin, prove
she's descended of bears, her totem, it's true.
And that German witch with the candy roof,
that was her ancestor too. If swans can rain
white rape from heaven, then what is a girl to do?
Believe her Indian eyes, her sly French smile,
her breast with its veins skim milk blue—
She is the myth that is true.

JILL BIALOSKY

from Fathers in the Snow

After father died
the love was all through the house
untamed and sometimes violent.
When the dates came we went up to our rooms
and mother entertained.
Frank Sinatra's "Strangers in the Night,"
the smell of Chanel No. 5 in her hair and the laughter.
We sat crouched at the top of the stairs.
In the morning we found mother asleep on the couch
her hair messed, and the smell
of stale liquor in the room.
We knelt on the floor before her,
one by one touched our fingers
over the red flush in her face.
The chipped sunlight through the shutters.
It was a dark continent
we and mother shared;
it was sweet and lonesome,
the wake men left in our house.

SUSAN FIRER

An Autobiography of an Angel

The trouble with being a woman, Skeezix, *is being a little girl in the first place.—Anne Sexton*

Every May on the Virgin's Holyday,
the whole congregation, in procession, moved
around our Santa Monica Catholic Church. We all
snaked past the football field, down Silver Spring
the business street, past Chicken-Delight, the bank,
the convent, the rectory, the bakery (always the same
wedding cake in the window), back across the
asphalt playground to the statue of the Blessed
Mary where we sang hymns
of love into the newly opened spring
windows and wind. And only because I was small
and blond and curly headed, I got to be a flower
crowned angel. I came after the Monsignor, the spring
vestmented priests and altar boys. FORGET THEM!
I got to wear the white satin angel
dress with the beautiful pastel ribbons.
And for one half hour, on an always sunny
May school day afternoon, in new white
patents and pastel-flowered-embroidered undies,
I was a hymn singing angel, carrying a bouquet of God's
flowers in my hands. An angel for a half hour
of procession I was not the child who always broke
windows with hardballs and red rubber suction-tipped
arrows, not the one who threw wet wash cloths
on hot lit light bulbs to hear explosions, not
the child who rifled through her parents' drawers,
not knowing what she was looking for. I was
not the child who hid her correction
shoes and bribed the boys for black high tops,
not the child who, from pretending to be asleep

(keep the eyelids relaxed, the breath even),
knew that Billy's mother was arrested for stealing
bobby pins from Kresge's, knew that the twins' father
had cocktails at lunchtime at Woolf's Island
with a woman who was not the twins' mother.
I was not the one who in winter lay in self-
made elaborately tunneled snow
forts until the whole world was white
except my child body I could float yellow,
not the child who prayed for a horse,
who hated her sister for always being
sick, who chewed red-wax lips and
stuck yellow kernel corn up her nose
until she couldn't breathe and the
fire department had to come to her house.
For twenty minutes of angel time I was
not the girl who wet her pants whenever
she laughed too hard, who hated the smell
of cancer in her Aunt Bea's hospital room,
who hated boys because they could be
altar boys, priests, or hobos. For twenty
minutes, I could forget the teenage boy
who had pulled me into my parents' garage
and oddly asked to suck the flat breast
spots on my eight year old body.
For twenty minutes of grade school time,
which for a child I'm sure is like dog years—
7 grade school child hours for every adult's one—
I could forget Mary Margaret, our 8th grade head
cheerleader, who had a brain tumor and had lost
all her beautiful white angel blond angel hair,
could not feed herself, and had to wear diapers.
For twenty minutes I could quit wondering
what the hell was behind Mr. Gunderson's, the
only male teacher in the school, & mine that year,
gray suit's plaid pant's zipper, anyway?
FOR I WAS AN ANGEL,
a May afternoon radium winged flower crowned angel,

deciding, like any other angel, whether to ever
turn back. Like most children I was
a saintly child piñata, filled and waiting
to break over the whole Goddamn village.

Movie Queens

The sisters cut them
from empty backdrops, propped them,
one atop a horse in a riding suit,
one at lunch on a cruise ship
skimming a bay in California.

Clusters of dolls leaned
against cement blocks,
a garden of pale faces
above shimmering lilts of cloth
and color, foxfur stoles,
ornaments of pearl and sequin.

The girls believed in what they could
become, as they vanished
into gowns, cashmere,
leaving sweating bodies, dim houses,
for a cold dry paradise.
Never having to earn a thing,
they'd stand, as clothes fell
from the sky in a rage of beauty.

DONNA MASINI

My Mother Makes Me a Geisha Girl

It is Halloween. 1962. Brooklyn.
It is late October. Afternoon light
seeps through venetian blinds.
I am eight years old. My mother is
making me up. My mother is making me
a geisha girl, rubbing white paint
across my face, my ears, down my throat.
Under her hands, my head
tilts. She works me over, licks
the tip of the Maybelline liner, marks
a black arch across my brow, adding
the years, filling in what she knows
should be there, the exotic
curve of the eye, hooking
toward the hairline, mole dot below
the lower lip. With a slim brush
she traces red into my lips, experience
paints in the sex. Blue shadows. Green shadows.
One hand twisting the hair from the nape
of my neck, she grips the bobby pins
in her mouth, talks through the narrow slit
in her teeth. *Hold still*, she says,
and *blot*, and *blink*.
She lightens, darkens, leaves
a pile of my mouths on crumpled Kleenex.
She is back

in 1947. Coney Island. A ride
called the Caterpillar, strapped by her date
in her seat. The lights go down, the puckered
larva begins to close, the boy
wraps his arm around her; she has waited
for this moment all her life: lipstick fresh,
stocking seams straight, her stomach flutters, she

stiffens, feels the vomit rising, she smiles
sinking, thinking *this is not right*, the Caterpillar
crawls through the tunnel, worms in the dark,
vomit rising, she backing away. This she tells me
as if to say *the body knows*. My body

does not know how to move in this pink
satin kimono she wraps about me. I choke
in the sweet cloud of her
Evening in Paris she sprays through my hair,
daubs at my throat. The body knows.
What my mother knows works on her, working on me.
Mincing steps, intricate hipwork. I can't
roll like the curve of my mother. She belts
me in, making a waist where no waist is.
My mother shows me how to be sexy. Shows
me my face in the oval mirror. I look

like a doll, all powder and posing,
wanting my own eyes back. How many faces I am.
I hunker down into a small knot,
a dark place where faces float
belly up like bloated fish. The girl
in the mirror is crying, her mother yelling
white paint smearing steamy shadows rolling
down mixing red blue black green.

WENDY MNOOKIN

Polio Summer

Best was the invalid, so we took turns
playing Colin. If Ellen in her wheelchair
was too tired, we pasted Trix on paper, orange boats
on a blue sea, and always a sun, round and yellow
and shining.

The cereal coating mixed with glue, smudged
shadows on Ellen's face. When she got too sick
for us to visit, no one wanted to be the patient
anymore, nursed to health with iced drinks and
Milky Ways,

although all she had to do was languish
on the backyard chaise. The week before
Ellen died, she floated in a tube at the beach
forbidden to us. What was it like,
drifting

weightless, legs sucked toward blue depths, face
tilted to a burning white sky? The summer of *The Secret*
Garden, mothers leaned close and whispered mysteries
we tried hard to understand. Later almost no one
passed by

the lemonade stand. Our fingers always sticky,
syrup tangled with the salty taste of sweat. The sun
shining, relentless, as it must have shone for her
that day at the beach, suspended between
two worlds.

CATHY SONG

The Grammar of Silk

On Saturdays in the morning
my mother sent me to Mrs. Umemoto's sewing school.
It was cool and airy in her basement,
pleasant—a word I choose
to use years later to describe
the long tables where we sat
and cut, pinned, and stitched,
the Singer's companionable whirr,
the crisp, clever bite of scissors
parting like silver fish a river of calico.

The school was in walking distance
to Kaimuki Dry Goods
where my mother purchased my supplies—
small cards of buttons,
zippers and rickrack packaged like licorice,
lifesaver rolls of thread
in fifty-yard lengths,
spun from spools, tough as tackle.
Seamstresses waited at the counters
like librarians to be consulted.
Pens and scissors dangled like awkward pendants
across flat chests,
a scarf of measuring tape flung across a shoulder,
time as a pincushion bristled at the wrist.
They deciphered a dress's blueprints
with an architect's keen eye.

This evidently was a sanctuary,
a place where women confined with children
conferred, consulted the oracle,
the stone tablets of the latest pattern books.
Here mothers and daughters paused in symmetry,
offered the proper reverence—

hushed murmurings for the shantung silk
which required a certain sigh,
as if it were a piece from the Ming Dynasty.

My mother knew there would be no shortcuts
and headed for the remnants,
the leftover bundles with yardage
enough for a heart-shaped pillow,
a child's dirndl, a blouse without darts.
Along the aisles
my fingertips touched the titles—
satin, tulle, velvet,
peach, lavender, pistachio,
sherbet-colored linings—
and settled for the plain brown-and-white composition
of polka dots on kettle cloth
my mother held up in triumph.

She was determined that I should sew
as if she knew what she herself was missing,
a moment when she could have come up for air—
the children asleep,
the dishes drying on the rack—
and turned on the lamp
and pulled back the curtain of sleep.
To inhabit the night,
the night as a black cloth, white paper,
a sheet of music in which she might find herself singing.

On Saturdays at Mrs. Umemoto's sewing school,
when I took my place beside the other girls,
bent my head and went to work,
my foot keeping time on the pedal,
it was to learn the charitable oblivion
of hand and mind as one—
a refuge such music affords the maker—
a pleasure of notes in perfectly measured time.

Small Gods

I thought my father was a god,
like all the other fathers down the block, floating
home in their gleaming cars filled with food
and thunder, manna and a terrible noise.
And the mothers were lesser gods, fragile
in their thin robes, their hair
so many multicolored clouds.
And we were small, barely human, huddled
half-naked like puppies on a rug, bathed
in the blue TV light, trying to be good.
We watched them from the corners of our eyes
as they swayed through the house on huge
fearless legs, or sat down slowly
with some large idea and a book.
I could not imagine the immense thoughts
they carried in their heads, their hearts
pumping like heavy machinery.
And maybe this was how it had to be, their silence
a rigid religion, a state of eternal grace
we could never know.
And of the animals I tended through those years,
skinny white mice and shivering birds, dogs
with their browbeaten eyes, the cat
who stared back at me with the glazed green irises
of an idiot savant. What did I know
of their terrors, their souls? Like the child I was,
I simply gave them names and fed them.
Day after day, I watched them grow.

ANGELA JACKSON

Blue Milk

Then we went to Bunny's house behind the church.
And played the Miracles Jesus never did,
over and over, memorizing the whorls of the songs
for the times when we'd know what they meant.
Our fingerprints all over the records, the records all in our
prints.
We poured that foreshadowed pain
into our hearts like blue milk
into curved blue bottles with deep stoppers.
Set them in our windows to wait for men who brought love
or not, but thirsty would
lean their fuzzy heads way back
exposing dark, strong necks and,
unstopping stoppers with sweat-staining fingers,
swallow all our blue smokey-miracle milk
till we could count our heart-
beats and breaks
in the deep sinkings and returns
of their adam's apples.

JEANNE BRYNER

Our Fathers

The day Joe Brodie fell into the acid pit
they say he screamed bigger than Texas.
When they pulled him out, his legs slid
off his waist like melted red candles.
He was crazy—yelling for his mama,
his wife, Martha Jane, and his kids
all at once. Just before he blacked out,
he clutched his foreman's stiff white shirt
and said, *Help me Tom, please . . . my legs.*

Joe Brodie died on the way to the hospital.
Our fathers finished their shift.
That night, my dad and his best friend, Ted,
went to Tony's Bar and got slop-the-hogs-
falling-down drunk. They talked about school
days back in Bobtown, Pa., and how yeast dough
smelled rising in their mama's kitchen,
how many bales they could toss in June,
and how they missed those sweet, lazy,
West Virginia nights.

And how hot Ohio was, hot and flat, and people
here called us hicks and ridge runners,
but by God, we knew how to work.
And our fathers never missed a shift;
salt stains scribbled lines on coveralls
like small boys print their names in dirt.

DIANE JARVENPA

The Other Language

The grownups line their bodies
on the hot upper bench of the sauna,
we children climb the bottom bench,
sit inside the thick membrane of heat.
Water hits the rocks
and we bow our heads,
receive the veil of steam.
Clouds take over the room in shapes
of ungodly heat and language.
Mary's father begins a long joke,
all the words lost on us kids
except for the punch line
paska housu—"shit pants."
Smiles spread before another blast of steam.

John's mother leans over to scrub his ears,
Finnish syllables spill from her mouth,
pebbles of nonsense through our minds as she
tells some piece of gossip to my mother.
As the room gets hotter
and the dialect further from our ken,
we descend the small knowledge of our bodies,
hearts banging against ribs,
blood rocking in our skulls,
forced beyond our natural breath
and lost inside our parents' other tongue.

All thoughts gone,
we run to the dock and jump,
the lake giving its great slap of cold.
In water we break our silence,
tattoo the air with sounds we understand,
loud dog-paddle races
and belly-flop competitions.

The adults, hair wet smooth,
sit on lawn chairs on the dock,
tip beer bottles in a circle
ready for the last of the sun.

Again their world returns
with the sounds of their music,
a language that is part of us
but one we will never be a part of;
the hard pain of their non-American childhood past,
entering kindergarten with no English words,
lonely bachelor uncles drinking
and shooting themselves in the barn,
the talk amongst the other townsfolk
of Finns and their drunken knife fights,
living in tiny backyard shacks,
the stigma assigned to being
wobblies or communists,
all making us a mute third generation.

That distant place our grandparents
stubbornly carried inside them in steerage
passes from their children's hands to ours.
The path is set for us,
but our eyes blink unsure
in the coming and present darkness.

LYNN EMANUEL

The Planet Krypton

Outside the window the McGill smelter
sent a red dust down on the smoking yards of copper,
on the railroad tracks' frayed ends disappearing
into the congestion of the afternoon. Ely lay dull

and scuffed: a miner's boot toe worn away and dim,
while my mother knelt before the Philco to coax
the detonation from the static. From the Las Vegas
Tonapah Artillery and Gunnery Range the sound

of the atom bomb came biting like a swarm
of bees. We sat in the hot Nevada dark, delighted,
when the switch was tripped and the bomb hoisted
up its silky, hooded, glittering, uncoiled length;

it hissed and spit, it sizzled like a poker in a toddy.
The bomb was no mind and all body; it sent a fire
of static down the spine. In the dark it glowed like the coils
of an electric stove. It stripped every leaf from every

branch until a willow by a creek was a bouquet
of switches resinous, naked, flexible, and fine.
Bathed in the light of KDWN, Las Vegas,
my crouched mother looked radioactive, swampy,

glaucous, like something from the Planet Krypton.
In the suave, brilliant wattage of the bomb, we were
not poor. In the atom's fizz and pop we heard possibility
uncorked. Taffeta wraps whispered on davenports.

A new planet bloomed above us; in its light
the stumps of cut pine gleamed like dinner plates.
The world was beginning all over again, fresh and hot;
we could have anything we wanted.

PAULA SERGI

Four on a Fold

Some summer nights in the early sixties,
in the middle of the country,
no ocean for thousands of miles
in either direction,
the air was everywhere heavy
like grandma's mothballed wool quilt,
navy as night
covering our faces, holding us down.
We should've been tired from play—
four square, seven steps around the house,
hopscotch drawn from the sharp side of a stone
on squares of concrete that marked
the edge of our front lawn.
Those nights we could stay up till nine,
but even after sunset no air moved.
We'd try to sleep
in the ten-by-twelve family room,
windows on three sides,
as if the screens themselves
would make a breeze.
Four on a fold-down couch
in short polyester pajamas
that stuck to our backs
waited for sleep,
for a breeze, for a father
who never came back to say goodbye.
I worried that maybe we'd all suffocate
before dawn, but we all grew up
one way or another
before we realized
how little air we'd had.

LESLIE ADRIENNE MILLER

Sleeping Out

When the new clover has sewn itself through
the grass, sturdy and pungent as an animal
presence, we know it is time. The boys
pitch their stern canvas affair
in Upton's field where it will stand
the summer, and girls passing it at sunrise
will wonder who or what sleeps late there
long for something like it, a space
marked out in the world, if only for a night.
We spirit the makings of our tents
from forbidden closets, drag the wads
of blankets from our beds into the air;
all our abundant need we find and pinch:
clothesline, porch mats, squat metal coolers,
hooks, bricks and tape to hold our edges down.
A larder too: a few pink wafer cookies,
damp white bread with sweating ovals of meat
wrapped in paper towel, even a wrinkled lemon
liberated from our mothers' kitchens.
We don't know what we'll need, and so
take everything, then hunt the ravine
for sticks thin enough to break across
our knees, strong enough to hold the romance
of a canopy against the stars.
                                                  The tents we make
are limp and list with breeze, half open
to the night. A spill of flowered bedroll
drifts in sleep toward the house
it came from, though the house is floating
off the dark edges of lawn, the fences
loosening, the cats tiptoeing along them,
trying to decide which world to jump on
when it all comes apart. Insects hum
in our hair and drink the cloying mix

of crushed clover, milk and girl
from our necks. One of us weeps,
afraid of the dark, and afraid to cross
the chasm that has opened between us
and her back door.
                                        At dawn, we know the boys
will come for us with their bats and firecrackers,
the cap guns that leave a breath of sulfur
in our hair, and this too, is something
we plan for and do not yet know we can
resent and retaliate against—someday
when we lie abed with them, refusing
to turn toward them in the collapse
of bedsheets and blasted desire,
we can simply wind our sweet, bitten
flesh with cover, and drag it all
home before dawn, leaving no more
than a crushed impression in the grass.

ELIZABETH ALEXANDER

Summertime

Where we live there are caged peacocks
in summertime, heavy in the heat,
bald-headed, dragging their tails, which,
once a season, they unfurl. Objects
wrinkle in the heat waves rising
from the pavement. A dead rat
in the back alley gets a proper
burial from a girl who can flip
her eyelids inside out, and at
the funeral I wear my white
go-go boots and sing "I Gotta Be Me."
We buy coverless comic books
cut-rate, impossibly red
vending machine pistachios
which stain our hands. A hydrant
illicitly opened, kids riding
the hard spray, caught in the rainbow
of water. On television,
Senators talk, talk talk.
A Wham-O Superball bounces
off a sidewalk crack and into
the cosmos. A red rubber planet
could bounce to the sky and stick.

JOSIE KEARNS

Satellite Father

for my older sister, Marilyn

When she was no longer eleven, in her party
dress of pink gingham and bows,
her father took her out like a debutante

for a spin and slowed the rusted Dodge
in front of a tavern, whose green neon
script said *Old Granddad* and *Malt Liquor.*

"I'm going to meet some people," he said,
"You stay here," a secret like a new cocktail
her head nodding below the half rolled down window

with its leaden chrome banding it
like the circlet on his cigar as he unwrapped
that quick as any present, headed away from her.

From the car seat she could play
with the mylar knobs on the radio
that didn't quite receive a station, kick

the plastic seat bottom sticking to the backs
of her legs like fly paper near their kitchen table.
Her patent leather heels tiny black pendulums

in 4/4 time, just missing each other, a rhythm
like the blues, lifting the backs of her small calves
off like BandAids, hugely slow at first, then faster

tempo, then tired kicking for nothing else to do
as 11:30, 12:15, 1:10, finally 2:15 whispers from
the luminescent green dial of the car clock

like the green cheese of the moon somewhere
outside, your father somewhere outside, the dark
of the car's black space, the only face she sees

until he staggers elliptically toward the Dodge
the orbit of one wingtip around the gravity
of cement curbs, pulling it down gingerly as

Neil Armstrong would later in her own
lifetime, that step for others, that non step bounce.
If it had been me in that six cylinder vehicle

swinging short legs, pounding the upholstery
with the fists of my heels, not knowing what
to do about him, saddening like the droop of pink

rose petals picked too early, in the echo of that
darkening street, all my thoughts as loud as comets.
If it had been me, reeling on the ride back

crisscrossing the center lines of streets like
equators, I couldn't have looked up at him
as if he were the first full moon in history

no tread of humans on his face. And I,
a stage of the earth, at which nothing much
had yet begun to happen.

JUDITH MONTGOMERY

Taking the Fences

Here's how I lived
when I was nine: wobbling
down River Road,
one hand on the handlebars,
one tucked against my ribs
cradling a book-freight
of tasty words—*spurt, crusty,*
petulant. Luminescent. Pride—
the soccer field banked to right,
the riverbank to left, rooted
in red alder, purple thistle, and
the trefoils of shine (poison

ivy through which Mrs. Brady's
Pontiac would pass, the brake
released by Bobby vrooming
at the wheel, with all three boys,
as I imagine, shining their grins
inside the glass-and-metal frame
that then plunged through the wire fence,
upended in the deep drown-hole
for twenty long minutes. The three
stripes clawing down the hood
spotted by their mailman—)

wobbling, as I said,
across Housatonic Bridge into town,
past Watson's aging soda fountain.
past the obelisk that scored the dead,
I skidded home at the snug brick
library where all the books I ever wanted
waited on the shelves. Mrs. Barton waved
and pointed me upstairs.

In the far nook my stool,
set eye-to-eye with Walter Farley.
All afternoon, I knocked my knees
together, rushed adazzle
on the backs of bays and chestnuts,
mouthing *forelock* and *withers*,
winding fingers in the manes
and setting my Black Stallion,
redfire Island Stallion,
to the dangerous fences
we always cleared.

from "A Cultural History of Fences"

Institutional Blue

In the welfare waiting room
  the woman cradles her jaw in her palm,
back molar aching in time

  to the piped-in music.

She's on her way to the county fair,
  free tickets and all her children
in tow, to soak in the sweat-sugared air.

  They don't know how sick

she feels, how each breath's cool sting
  bends her double in the plastic seat.
She tests the tooth with her tongue.

  Beside her, all in a row, the children

swing their legs, and finger nine-month-old
  magazines, and laugh. The clerk
lets them know with her eyes, the snap of a folder,

  that they are too loud, again.

My brother calls back this day
  as one more in a chain of embarrassments,
when my mother, to keep us calm while waiting,

  made up games and begged us: Be sweet.

The Health Department posters plastered the walls
  with civic warnings and sickly children.
We prayed for handfuls of dollars

—at night, that helped us get to sleep—

and we lined up for the stamps
that fed us tuna and Spam, that emaciated chicken
drying beneath the butcher's blue lamp.

Then the door closed behind us with a click:

the hot car ride, the money, food, lights,
sweat of the fair, a tired conjunction
of desires. And the carnies' faces, my mother's tight

voice: We won't end up like them. That sticks.

White Lies

The lies I could tell,
when I was growing up
light-bright, near-white,
high-yellow, red-boned
in a black place,
were just white lies.

I could easily tell the white folks
that we lived uptown,
not in that pink and green
shanty-fied shot-gun section
along the tracks. I could act
like my homemade dresses
came straight out of the window
of *Maison Blanche.* I could even
keep quiet, quiet as kept,
like the time a white girl said
(squeezing my hand) *now*
we have three of us in this class.

But I paid for it every time
Mama found out.
She laid her hands on me,
then washed out my mouth
with Ivory soap. *This*
is to purify, she said,
and cleanse your lying tongue.
Believing her, I swallowed suds
thinking they'd work
from the inside out.

KELLY NORMAN ELLIS

Girl

you wore blue pedal pushers and polka dot tops
saturday mornings
when sun still spoke
through a screenless window above the sink
and the radio rested on its ledge
holding the jive of a dj papa
"the sounds of soul w-o-k-j"
girl
nestled between some newly womanish hips
your hands submerged in lemon joy and breakfast dishes
while the bottoms of bare feet
slid
slopped and
ponied
to four tops
impressions and
dramatics
you were a girl with dixie peach bangs
hugging pink sponge rollers
and cashmere bouquet sprinkled
in the crease of not long opened breasts
who dreamed of boys
talking in poems
and moving in beauty like marvin gaye
will you remember this girl when you are a woman
will you remember to love her when she dances
across your dreams and kisses you
like a daughter
on the lips?

2
The Age of Unlimited Possibilities

HARRIET LEVIN

The Christmas Show

While my youngest sister lies
on a cold cellar floor
in a house whose broken windows hold back nothing
and three boys pin down her shoulders
and force their way past her belt buckle, I am watching
The Christmas Show at Radio City Music Hall, seeing
a full moon accentuate the otherworldliness
of children dressed as elves, skating snowmen
and cardboard reindeer.
While my youngest sister lies on her back, stripped naked,
and three boys, one at a time, move over her, I am
    applauding
when an entire row of girls
wearing bright red bathing suits
fleeced with white fur
kick open their legs, the whole house applauds
at that moment. While my youngest sister looks into the
    dark
wide pupils she will look into
for the rest of her life, the boys
who prick her throat with a knife
feel only a momentary pleasure.
And just when I think The Christmas Show is over,
the curtain opens once more
with sheep, straw and stars
and the story of the nativity begins,
of a birth with no sex in it.
A real live camel is led across the stage
in a caravan with sheiks, children, and beggars
waiting to be touched and saved,
but at that moment
my mother is rushing to open the front door
my sister pounds

and pounds on, blood on her face, her lips
swollen, her cheek swollen, her
eyes swollen, having seen enough.

DONNA HILBERT

Craving

I broke the long stems
of dry spaghetti
into worm-sized pieces
that I ate as I watched
cartoons on TV:
Baby Huey in his tiny diaper,
Porky and Petunia Pig.
I popped the round top
from the Hershey's chocolate can,
spooned the unsweetened
powder into my mouth.
Mom was pregnant then.
At my eleventh birthday party,
Dad patted her belly,
bragged to my friends
that he'd *blown up that balloon.*
It was the beginning of summer.
My friends had begun to kiss boys,
steal candy and cigarettes
from Vons.
I spent the long afternoons
lying on the floor,
cartoons flickering silently
on the black and white TV,
the cord of the telephone
wrapped around my arm,
whispers of the high school boy
I knew from the park
slipping into my ear.
I ate the skin
from the tips of my fingers,
from the tops of my toes
until they bled.

I didn't know then
what was bitter,
as my life spilled out around me,
fine powder from a dark brown tin.

KYOKO MORI

Barbie Says Math Is Hard

As a boy, I'd still have asked
why Jack must spend exactly
two dollars at the corner store.
Give him a coin purse is as
good an answer as five apples
and two oranges. Also: would
he bake the apples into pies
or cobblers, save the orange peel
in glass jars to spice up his
tea or cake? If his father
paints their house with Mr. Jones,
which man will take the peaks and
why? Would the raspberry beetles
swarm over wet paint? Why is
Mr. Jones slower than his
neighbor? If x equals y,
is it like putting apples into
cole slaw, the way a tomato
is really a fruit? None of my
dolls talked or grew hair. In
third grade, Satsuki and I
traded our Barbies' limbs so
mine could flex her left biceps
while hers sat cross-legged
raising one stiff arm
like a weapon. If Satsuki has
daughters, she might remember
the grasshoppers we caught,
how we cupped two hands together
into crooked globes to
hear them rattling inside like
a small motor. She would tell
her daughters: Yes, math was hard,
but not because we were girls.

ALLISON JOSEPH

Traitor

What did that girl on the playground mean
when she hissed *you ain't black* at me,

pigtails bouncing, her hands
on her bony hips? She sucked her teeth,

stared at me with such contempt
that I wanted to hide in my mother's

skirts, wanted to scurry to my house's
hall closet, safe among the great

dark coats. *You talk funny*, she said,
all proper, as if pronunciation

was a sin, a scandal, a strike
against the race only a traitor

would perform, an Uncle Tom sellout.
Somehow I'd let her down by not

slurring, I'd failed her by not
letting language laze on its own,

its sound unhurried. I'd said
isn't rather than *ain't*,

called my mother *mom* instead of
momma, pronounced *th* distinctly

so no one would confuse *them*
with *dem*, *those* with *dose*.

Your momma talk that funny?
The girl demanded, her face

in my face now, her nose
inches from mine, her eyes

lit by something near hate,
but more ferocious, a kind

of disgust mixed with pity,
disdain. *We're from Canada,*

I said, and the girl's eyes
went wide, as if I'd said

cantaloupe or *harpoon,*
or some nonsense word like

abracadabra. There must not be
no black folks in Canada then,

she sneered, leaning in further,
pushing on my chest with one

bony finger, pinning me there
like a bug to a fly screen,

pressing me so hard that
my lower lip started to tremble

on its own, a sign of weakness
she laughed a mocking, heavy

laugh at, telling me *go on and cry,*
white girl, cry till your momma

can hear, pushing me so I toppled
onto my back, ripping the pants

my mother warned me not to rip.
She stood over me, laughing

like she'd just seen the world's
best clown, laughing though I

was just as dark as she,
my hair in the same

nappy plaits, my skin
the same rough brown.

MARILYN CHIN

First Lessons

dedicated to the character 好 *or "goodness"*

1
I got up; a red shiner bloomed
like a rose in my eye. She said,
"A present fit for a queen . . . served
by the hand which fed you, soothed you
and presently, slaps you to your senses.

"Your goddess of Mercy has spoken."

She ran, blonde hair ablaze,
dust settling on asphalt.

I did it again.
I got up from the blood and the mud
crying like a bullcalf,
not for the wound but for the dress.

2
This is how I remember *goodness.*

A woman whose lipstick smells of lilac leans over a child.
She says, "Have you been good?"
The child, kneels like a supplicant,
looks up, whispers, "always."

3
Dust we are made, dust we leave behind—
The dress shall be clean no matter the circumstance.
My friend; my foe, wearing worn Levis and a T-shirt,
hides in the schoolyard, now, with her black labrador.

4

I learned *goodness* before I learned my name.
I learned the strokes, their order, but never the message:

that the good shall never rise from their knees is my
river-to-cross.

JULIA KASDORF

Catholics

for Julia

In third grade all the girls got confirmed
and had their ears pierced. They flaunted
those dingy threads that hung from their lobes,
telling how the ice stung, how the cartilage crunched
when the needle broke through, how knots
in the thread had to be pulled through the holes,
one each day, like a prayer on the rosary.

At recess I turned the rope
while Michelle skipped and spun and counted to ten,
and a scapular leapt from the neck of her dress.
She dangled that pale pink ribbon,
a picture of the Blessed Mother on one end
and the Sacred Heart on the other,
saying, "This is my protection, front and back."
That was when I called them Catholic
and said, "Your people killed my people;
your priests threw a man into a river,
tied in a sack with a dog, a cat, a rooster, a snake,
think how they scratched and bit going down,
think how they drowned. Your priests
burned holes in the tongues of our preachers,
and put pacifists naked in cages
to starve and rot while the birds
pecked off their flesh."

Michelle and Vicki and Lisa just looked at me,
the jump rope slack as a snake
at our feet. But in my memory
I want those girls with the fine bones and dark eyes
to speak up:

those priests were not me,
those martyrs weren't you,
and we have our martyr stories, too.
I want to take their slim girl-bodies into my arms
and tell them I said it only because
I wanted to wear a small, oval medal
I could pull from my T-shirt to kiss
before tests. I wanted a white communion dress,
and to pray with you
to your beautiful Blessed Mother in blue.

JACKIE BARTLEY

Hershey's

My mother carried a Hershey bar with almonds
in her hinged purse, thrown in with wallet and loose change,
with car keys, lipstick, compact, pill containers,
coupons, old grocery lists, bus schedules, a lint cloud
of Kleenex, combs, white cotton gloves.

She carried it everywhere—department stores, restaurants,
grade school on parents' day, the airport
where she met my father after his week-long business trips.
As if her life were in that purse
                                        or grew from it like Venus
rising from the sea, love from its practical source.

Once in every season—before school began when plaid wool
hung from racks, made our eyes dance inside Gimbel's,
at Christmas when life-size dolls in green velvet,
powdered snow in their hair, skated on mirrors in
   Kauffmann's
window displays, in spring among Easter lilies and
   hyacinths,
and in the chlorine summers of Catalina turquoise—
we went downtown by bus to shop all day.

When we finished, we waited in front of a bakery
for the 78B to take us home.
                                        Sometimes we bought
their tea cookies: thumbprints iced with green and pink
and lemon yellow pastels, or spice gems—maple drizzle
over gingered raisin cakes.
                                        But only once, when the day
had been especially long, when the city's soot and gravel
burned behind our eyelids, she opened her purse and
   produced
the Hershey bar.

I still remember its sweet
meditative ooze,
the dazzle of almond, like nothing I've eaten since.

Some days now, I feel as if I'm walking in the clutter
of that great clasped purse, tracing a brailled path
that sends me circling the same stretch of darkness
over and over.
And then it is there, a sure
simple thing,
the sweet thin flicker of memory like a promise
wrapped and waiting.

LONNIE HULL DuPONT

Looking for God

As a little girl, I marveled
at Johnny Cash's crying songs, wondered
about him shooting that man in Reno
just to watch him die. I was curious
about Patsy Cline falling to pieces, about
what might cause that since
no one ever went to pieces in my house
even when they were thrown into walls.
And when Johnny Cash rock-a-billied in jail
and Patsy Cline fell from the sky,
pieces of her glittery clothing
scattered around a burning cornfield,
I became a seeker looking for God.
From a stack of 45s left by my teenage cousins
I heard a Sam Cooke B-side, and then
I knew God had found me, had delivered to me
my personal hymn in his textured Memphis voice.
I saw God had been around, he knew something
about jail and pieces of a life that could no longer
be snapped back into place. And God may have been
shot to death one night in a motel brawl,
but he lived on inside me,
his most holy spirit soothing my wide-eyed
pony-tailed self by singing *Summertime*
and the livin' is easy . . . .
My little-girl logic understood that
when God sang about high cotton,
he really meant looming rows of June corn.
He sang of my affluent stepfather, my lovely
dreaming mother in that song, making
some sense of it for me, *hush little baby,*
don't you cry. And when he told me
I would fly out of there one day,

I believed! All I had to do was
turn on the hi-fi and
I was born again and again.

ANGELA JACKSON

Faith

Longlegged boys leapt from rooftop to rooftop.
The dark between their legs widening as they spread.

We never questioned the quiet behind the house until the
  boys made
their legs scissors and cut it. What we thought could not be
  cut,
as it was made from the stones on the floor of the alley
  below,
the eaves above the garages that slanted, so standing there
  was an
art
and lifting off
a greater one.

They could have fallen, but they would not have fallen.
Gifted by heaven to lose gravity in the dark, gain grace
enough to make girls weep to follow, all of us, even looking
  up,
born anew in midair, no longer grievingly human, mute.
The wind in our mouths. Each breath big, sweetened with
  amazement.

Once black boys, innocent as angels, leapt from rooftop to
  rooftop.
Full splits on a floor of dark air, each time a happy ending.
Isn't that enough?

LIZ ABRAMS-MORLEY

In Levittown, Before Her Mother's Vanity

wearing Mama's hat, white crepe
rose centered flatly
above pencil-smudged eyes,
                slyly, she puckers.
You know how to whistle, don't you?
Bogart's honey whispers
like snow falling in her
brain. *You just put your lips*
                together and blow.
Cole Porter on her mother's
radio and her hips can't help
swiveling so the line she draws
up the back of one white calf
                and thigh snakes
as if the stocking it meant
to replace got twisted at the foot.
Shit, she's saying, though
she's been told no 1930s lady
                would curse
that way. It's 1958 and she's
practically a baby, stuck in fifth
grade where other girls appear
                content, wide
white sashes slashed over plaid,
stupidly playing Mom kisses
Dad in their Amana kitchens,
                wishing Ward
Cleaver for a husband, a taffy
and white Lassie or Lad, a lifetime
in which to have two
sons, one named Ricky or David.
                It's ages before
the real Ricky sings kissing songs,

gets jazzed, gets killed in a crash,
a decade before her favorite
            stars stumble
onto New York stages, brain-
fried or wrinkled, to lip-synch
sex and steam. This is the time
of Dick and Jane, men in wingtips
            who choose dead over
red, scrubbed virgins innocent
as Mother's white formica.
            Hy-gee-nic
her teacher, Mr. Fagen says, and begs
permission to wash
her mouth out with soap whenever
she slips into Lauren
Bacall's sultry *"well, just*
            screw it all,"
while other girls nervously study
ordered desk tops, clean, trimmed
nails, the boys all stare and squirm.
            They all want her
to disappear or pull her hair
tight in a ponytail, wear polished
saddle shoes. She can't tell them
            she wants
Cole Porter songs, longs to grin
like she saw Mama grin,
            spied through a crack
one afternoon, when she thought herself
alone in this room, before
this glass. Mama wearing nothing but
            this wide-brimmed hat
splashing lilac cologne on her inside
thighs, splashing and humming,
and smiling a smile like even
their neighbors with modernized
            kitchens never
seemed to smile. It's years before

Jackie's polite pillboxes, years
before this child sees her mother needs
    one more gin
to face lunch. It's 1958
and still she believes
a new life can be
    pulled from a hat.

KATE GLEASON

The Age of Unlimited Possibilities

My sister and I, being girls,
wasted the better part
of our childhoods
practicing to be women.

Every fall, our lawn swelled
with the colors of singed orange,
crayon yellow, maroon,
the brilliant ruin we raked
into the floor plans of leaf houses,
elaborate ranches with dream kitchens,
conversation areas, sunken living rooms.

It was the 50s. The shelf life
of lunch meats had been extended
to an unheard-of two months.
There was no end to the possibilities.
Test pilots had broken the sound barrier,
filling the sky with a synthetic thunder
we could feel as much as hear,
like an explosion underwater.

Housewives in smart A-line dresses
happily vacuumed with their new uprights,
rearranged their sectional furniture,
and invented creative mingling
between Jell-O and miniature marshmallows.

World War II was behind us,
the legion of evil ones again stymied,
forced to retreat, like a glacier,
but leaving in its wake
a mawkish and exaggerated innocence.

It was the 50s and I'd just learned
that a girl could not so much as hope
to become president, owing to the fact
that women had their time of the month
when they might do something unthinking.

It was the 50s,
"the age of unlimited possibilities,"
just as World War I had been
"the war to end all wars,"
and like a lot of families back then,
we'd hunkered in
behind our white picket fence,
trying to still believe
that what words said
was what they meant.

NATASHA TRETHEWEY

Collection Day

Saturday morning, Motown
forty-fives and thick seventy-eights
on the phonograph, window fans
turning light into our rooms,
we clean house to a spiral groove,
sorting through our dailiness—
washtubs of boiled-white linens,
lima beans soaking, green as luck,
trash heaped out back for burning—
everything we can't keep,
make new with thread or glue.

Beside the stove, a picture calendar
of the seasons, daily scripture,
compliments of the Everlast Interment
Company, one day each month marked
in red—PREMIUM DUE—collection visit
from the insurance man, his black suits
worn to a shine. In our living room
he'll pull out photos of our tiny plot,
show us the slight eastward slope,
all the flowers in bloom now, how neat
the shrubs are trimmed, *and see here,*
the trees we planted are coming up fine.

We look out for him all day, listen
for the turn-stop of wheels
and rocks crunching underfoot.
Mama leafs through the Bible
for our payment card—June 1969,
the month he'll stamp PAID
in bright green letters, putting us
one step closer to what we'll own,
something to last: patch of earth,
view of sky.

Queens, 1963

Everyone seemed more American
than we, newly arrived,
foreign dirt still on our soles.
By year's end, a sprinkler waving
like a flag on our mowed lawn,
we were melted into the block,
owned our own mock Tudor house.
Then the house across the street
sold to a black family.
Cop cars patrolled our block
from the Castellucci's at one end
to the Balakian's on the other.
We heard rumors of bomb threats,
a burning cross on their lawn.
(It turned out to be a sprinkler.)
Still the neighborhood buzzed.
The barber's family, Haralambides,
our left side neighbors, didn't want trouble.
They'd come a long way to be free!
Mr. Scott, the retired plumber,
and his plump midwestern wife,
considered moving back home
where white and black got along
by staying where they belonged.
They had cultivated our street
like the garden she'd given up
on account of her ailing back,
bad knees, poor eyes, arthritic hands.
She went through her litany daily.
Politely, my mother listened—
¡Ay, Mrs. Scott, qué pena!
—her Dominican good manners
still running on automatic.
The Jewish counselor next door,

had a practice in her house;
clients hurried up her walk
ashamed to be seen needing.
(I watched from my upstairs window,
gloomy with adolescence,
and guessed how they too must have
hypocritical old world parents.)
Mrs. Bernstein said it was time
the neighborhood opened up.
As the first Jew on the block,
she remembered the snubbing she got
a few years back from Mrs. Scott.
But real estate worried her,
our houses' plummeting value.
She shook her head as she might
at a client's grim disclosures.
Too bad the world works this way.
The German girl playing the piano
down the street abruptly stopped
in the middle of a note.
I completed the tune in my head
as I watched *their* front door open.
A dark man in a suit
with a girl about my age
walked quickly into a car.
My hand lifted but fell
before I made a welcoming gesture.
On her face I had seen a look
from the days before we had melted
into the United States of America.
It was hardness mixed with hurt.
It was knowing she never could be
the right kind of American.
A police car followed their car.
Down the street, curtains fell back.
Mrs. Scott swept her walk
as if it had just been dirtied.
Then the German piano commenced
downward scales as if tracking

the plummeting real estate.
One by one I imagined the houses
sinking into their lawns,
the grass grown wild and tall
in the past tense of this continent
before the first foreigners owned
any of this free country.

JENNIFER LAGIER

1958 Fruit Cutting Shed

It's where I learned
about french kisses, cruising,
and the Ronettes,
that cutting shed of crimped tin
above a dirt floor.

My grandmother
helps me complete the blank lines
upon my first time card,
nine years old,
plastic apron, new knife
and sack lunch of salami
clamped in sweaty hands.

As agreed, I earn
twenty-five cents
per immense box of freestones.
Money for school clothes
and good practice
learning how to work,
my mother explains.

Children stand on pallets
and slice sticky fruit
as the sulfur fumes sting.
The ten year old shed boy,
my future husband,
comes to our table,
uncovers its skeletal frame,
removes layers of peach halves
when I shout "Trays away!"

June, July, August.
My fingers harden,
strengthen and bleed.

JUDY BELSKY

Hula Hoop Summer

Everyone has one the summer I am eleven.
Even the Clairol blonde triplets
on the Ed Sullivan Show.

My father and I see them
at the Five and Dime.
They remind him of the hoops
he pushed with a stick
as a child in England.
Between aisles of toys and work boots
I try one out, keep it moving
over my hips. How-things-come-around,
he muses, paying for it.

When my mother sees the two
ninety-eight tag dangling from it,
her eyes, mouth, and nostrils form
a series of O's crowned by the
dark mezzalunas of her eyebrows.
She spaces her words to the rhythm
of precisely sliced carrots:
You-always-could-keep-that-man-wound-
around-your-baby-finger.

All summer I sway on the grass,
learning how things come around,
how the earth rotates
on a central axis,
how hips defy gravity.

JEANNE BRYNER

Sunday Morning

My Mama is blotting her red lipstick
and the tired Bible waits on our gray
kitchen table; we have a nickel
for the collection plate. We whine
because Ben gets to carry the nickel.
Ben will drop it, we say. Mama is firm.
We wear strawberry pink dresses and the boys wear
blue sailor suits; bacon grease is Mama's scent.

Nancy scrapes cornmeal mush into Sam's bowl;
he gulps. Glass is broken in the trash
and bloodstains dry on our green couch.
Sunday morning means the end of Saturday night
pain. Mama is in her aqua seersucker skirt;
she is a wave from the ocean. She presses
pancake make-up over her left shiner;
her ice bag sweats on the toilet lid.

My Mama is singing softly beneath her wide-brimmed
straw hat, *Oh, come to the church in the wildwood,*
and Mrs. Harvey points at my Mama and the brown suit
preacher pounds his Methodist pulpit
screaming about hell's fury. . . .

My Mama's hair is the color of honey;
she quiets my brothers. My Mama's pancake make-up
is melting from all this talk of hell.
Her left eye is a slit under a purple avalanche,
and purple is the color for the church;
the color for royalty.

Apollo

We pull off
to a road shack
in Massachusetts
to watch men walk

on the moon. We did
the same thing
for three two one
blast off, and now

we watch the same men
bounce in and out
of craters. I want
a Coke and a hamburger.

Because the men
are walking on the moon
which is now irrefutably
not green, not cheese,

not a shiny dime floating
in a cold blue,
the way I'd thought,
the road shack people don't

notice we are a black
family not from there,
the way it mostly goes.
This talking through

static, bouncing in space-
boots, tethered
to cords is much
stranger, stranger

even than we are.

DORIANNE LAUX

Twelve

Deep in the canyon, under the red branches
of a manzanita, we turned the pages
slowly, seriously, as if it were a holy text,
just as the summer before we had turned
the dark undersides of rocks to interrupt
the lives of ants, or a black stinkbug
and her hard-backed brood.
And because the boys always came,
even though they weren't invited, we never
said anything, except Brenda who whispered
Turn the page when she thought we'd seen enough.
This went on for weeks one summer, a few of us
meeting at the canyon rim at noon, the glossy
magazine fluttering at the tips of our fingers.
Brenda led the way down, and the others
stumbled after blindly, Martin
always with his little brother
hanging off the pocket of his jeans, a blue
pacifier stuck like candy in his mouth.
Every time he yawned, the wet nipple
fell out into the dirt, and Martin, the good brother,
would pick it up, dust it with the underside
of his shirt, then slip it into his own mouth
and suck it clean. And when the turning
of the pages began, ceremoniously, exposing
thigh after thigh, breast after beautiful,
terrible breast, Martin leaned to one side,
and slid the soft palm of his hand
over his baby brother's eyes.

KATE SONTAG

When Memory Is a Gardenia in Your Stepmother's Hair

You'd like to hear her voice again, sympathetic
as a cello finally reaching you one Sunday
through the noon siren: "Poor child," she says,
"You're growing up with no sense of infinity."

But under the kitchen table where you've taken
to hiding in the same somersault position
practiced during drills at school like a body
ready to roll down a hill at a moment's notice,

the word "infinity" heartlessly blooms
its mushroom cloud inside you,
pale and swollen and sudden
as her oldest boy's hands. You think

of *his* hands as she offers you her own,
how on weekends when you visit
he wakes you at dawn while everyone else is
asleep. There is no mistaking the rosy girl-

trail his fingers take in and out of you
for any other pain. As if it will last forever,
whatever he is doing still floats to the surface
of your skin, prickly as the spines of

the blowfish suspended by strings
and staring down at you from the ceiling
of his bedroom the day of the wedding.
Soon, perhaps, their rude mouths will be

stuffed with her favorite tropical blossoms
that perfume the driveway (the ones she's raised
from seed) silencing her bittersweet claim on you.
Even now, when you'd like to picture her

saving you from the end of the world
in her own house, her yearning for a daughter
is no match for a teenage son's revenge,
lingering invisibly beneath the same canopy

he helps you hold upright: outside where guests
surround the *chupah*, a wineglass shatters under your father's
foot to commemorate the destruction of the Temple,
a gardenia beginning to brown in his bride's hair

is the first and last stepflower on earth.

JUDITH HOUGEN

Coming of Age

We skidded up in late afternoon to the lake cottage,
hot, steel bucket in the back seat bulging
with wild strawberries, the cologne of July
blown in our hair. Engine off, the day
squeezed close again like the sweaty arms of my old aunt.
The women buzzed the bucket to the kitchen in a rush
of blue aprons. My nails, hemmed with russet horseshoes,
dug out hulls, while my mother's voice
rose clear as the scent of fresh tablecloths
snapped open in the dining room. After dinner,
the berries waded in heavy cream, we relaxed
in a humid breeze barely breathing off Lake Minnetonka,
the sky sinking into a last cup of lukewarm coffee.
At twelve, time reinventing my body, I was old enough
to sit amid the tribe in poppy-print dresses
and red-faced toenails. From our patch of porch light,
I heard waves slapping the shore, realized
even darkness is comforted by the talk of women,
the sweetness raised in the pink lines of their hands.

HEID ERDRICH

Creation

I

That March we were thirteen,
best friends dressed as twins, in love
the way young girls love mirrors,
anything to better see ourselves.
But any lingering look from any male
broke us open fiercely, too early
like the dandelions we tore—green buds
opening to the yellow, unformed flowers.

II

In the heat beaten late July garden
of the Lutheran Home for Girls, the arc
of her pregnancy strains to the sun.
Thick air drapes about her, she wears it.
A neat garden rolls out for her. A path
beside a birdbath ends in knee-deep columbine.
I imagine Eve there, Eve who likes gardens.
She pinches the flowers' honey-filled tips,
brushes past sunflowers who spend their whole
enraptured day bending, like lovers, for the light—
She shakes pollen from the seed heads, claps
her hands, watches yellow clouds rise up, disperse.
Then Eve sings, holding out notes long
and clear as love. But my friend hears
only the noise of the garden—
the vibration of pistil and stamen,
the loud love-making petals,
every plant humming for release.

3
The Long Dark Dialogue

Apron

If she wore one, she'd be at the strings with a vengeance. Clip them clear off with cuticle scissors from her Revlon manicure kit, or set a match to them like a fuse and blow off the stupid bow.

Actually, there were no more bows after 1957, after the third baby in six years. No strings for her: she and the girls from bridge club began to wear cocktail aprons. Not even aprons, really, just flaps of flashy fabric on a waistband that snapped closed—no bib, no pockets, no sash. Strictly decoration: holiday motifs, Moderne geometrics.

She never wore a housedress or a housecoat or even a bathrobe after she pitched that nubby pink one in the rag pile the day the baby spit up in her hair and she threw his bottle in the trash for good. She established strict routines after that and administered with a sure hand. Dad said she was born to command—a compliment that offended her, wanting, like she did, lots of distance between the goddamn olive-drab war and her house and her children. And he *was* wrong, way off the mark. She was no drill sergeant. She was born to rule.

Queen for a Day: we watched it on TV every afternoon after school. Pathetic country women who couldn't afford a washing machine or an icebox, begging for a helping hand, pitching pity like circus barkers till the audience applause meter put an end to their misery. We sat on the rug, rapt at the sight of weeping mothers in threadbare aprons, flapping fistfuls of photos at the camera like a bad hand of poker. Pictures of hollow-eyed children, gaunt and slovenly on a rickety porch in some god-forsaken dusty place. Tugging at her, always tugging at her. But her plea—no matter what the merchandise—was always for *my precious children.*

Such excitement, parties. She had the food—a crown roast, whimsical hors d'oeuvres, oddball drinks!—ready by five. Then the bath, the hair, the makeup application after which she could not be approached. We could watch, sitting in a row at the end of her bed, as she dressed. She never hesitated or wavered before the row of dressy dresses; knew exactly what she wanted and put it on confidently. Perched before the vanity, she applied the final touches—a dab of Intimate cologne, the double strand of pearls, hair spray—then stepped into her ankle-strap high heels and turned toward us.

The skirt a sweep of midnight blue taffeta atop layers of petticoats, extending her personal periphery a full two feet. The strapless bodice and oh! the rigging underneath that allowed her to swoop and twirl half naked without a care. She was exquisite, serene. We begged to light her cigarette with the crystal lighter.

Kiss me goodnight, now, before I put on my lipstick. We leaned in, careful to avoid the crisp skirt, the lacquered hair. We bent for our kiss, our brief waft of her—smoke, perfume, shampoo, leather. *If you're real good, I'll tell the ladies to put their minks on your bed.*

DONNA MASINI

Getting Out of Where We Came From

I was born in Brooklyn.
Even the birds were dingy
and the dark courtyard between
buildings filled with grimy light
like the lit up inside of a pumpkin.
There we could be frantic.
There we could stamp and spin
or fall down pretending to be dead.
It is still the place my father loves.
I see him: slicing meats,
stampeding streets in wild teenage goodboy crowds,
so near to me, on the lip of my dream
green workclothes still oil the air
of my bedroom, saturate the walls.
He works hard for you seven days a week.
In 1963 grease-soaked, shadowed, we ferried the harbor
to a new duplex. The model home.
Barbecues, mortgages. *Where will we get the money?*
The bridge went up. The basement flooded.
Up to our knees in water we bailed and bailed.
In their yards the neighbors laughed
and drank and shook their heads, *Too bad
they didn't know the house was built on a swamp.*

Crystal Lake

I caught crawdads and let them go. Baited hooks with my grandfather, watched iridescent dragonflies fly between heaven and hell. I was restless in adolescent heat, wandered the rocky banks of Crystal Lake. No one else there: too hot, too humid, except for the cool lake of the fish, water moccasins slicing through the invisible current, a turtle's nose above water, and my grandfather pulling another bass out of the underworld. I watch it flip and leap in the cutting air. The gills bleeding this gift of air onto the gritty rocks. I say stop this suffering, but my mouth evokes nothing in the flat, wet blanket of noon. I am too curious of my own death, riding the sling between my newborn hips, to pay respect or help. We take the boat back through the finger of the lake. Caves echo each paddle stroke, suck the ripple in and turn them into our own voices calling to us from blind halls. Come home, come home, the meaning feeding the crumbling guilt at the sudden turn of my body. Bats fly at perfect random from the limestone cliffs, follow the invisible moon. I don't remember any words, but the shushing of the sun through dried grass, nibble of carp at the bottom of the boat, the slow melting of my body. My grandfather towed us through the lake. We skimmed over mythical fish he once caught, over fish who were as long as rainbows after the coming storm.

REBECCA McCLANAHAN

Passion Week, 1966

In the sanctuary of fundamental *no*'s
so much was not allowed.
What was left pressed hard
to free itself, the way
even a modest breast, laced
into a bustier, surprises

with dollops of flesh.
It was the week of Christ's
suffering and release. A ceiling fan
paddled the heat as voices of boys
in the pew behind me wandered
the lower octaves. One tenor had legs so long

he could stretch his feet to mine,
which slipped out of white pumps
at first touch and stayed
through hymns and prayers
and the miracle of bread
into flesh. The altar portrait

was a savage Jesus—wilderness hair
and shoulders bare and muscled,
the kind of body God the Father
might have kneaded from clay.
Parents nodded in their accustomed pews
while those of us cast in new bodies

leaned into the story of the son's
earthly side, the women
who loved him. His mother, of course.
The sisters of Lazarus. The whore
who annointed his feet with kisses
and tears, dried them with her hair

and rubbed oils that might have been sold,
the disciples said, to feed the poor.
And Christ, dusty and tired
and not long for this world, rebuked
her rebukers, claiming a higher charity
and suffering the woman to do it.

ALISON TOWNSEND

Supplies

Because I believed my stepmother hated me,
because I'd sat alone in the school auditorium
the day all the sixth grade mothers came
and watched a film called *Growing Up and Liking It*
with their girls, I didn't tell her anything
when it arrived for the first time,
but went straight from the bus to my room
and sat with my legs clenched
around the institutional-sized Kotex
the school nurse had safety-pinned
to my stained Carter's panties.

"I assume you have supplies?" she'd said,
yanking up the panties so hard it hurt.
I didn't, but lied, knowing it wasn't
a question by the way she avoided my eyes,
hoping I'd find an answer in the dog-eared
booklet with anatomical drawings,
pictures of pretty girls
with perfectly combed hair
going swimming or riding,
and cheery captions urging me to
"Remember, you can do all the things you usually do!"

I had no supplies.
No quilted pink box like the one
my friend Caroline showed me,
tucked in a drawer with her mother's brassieres,
the little pads stacked, neat and white
as piles of linen, tampons in crackling paper,
("for when I'm older," she whispered,
touching them with a reverent hand)
and the stretchy, lace-trimmed belts

in different colors like ads I had seen
in *Tiger Beat* for Frederick's of Hollywood.

I'd done my reading, but I wasn't prepared.
And so sat in my room, aching, while the bright
arterial red turned a deep rust that smelled
strange and smoky, alive and dead
at the same time, praying it would end.
But it kept flowing, no matter what I did,
until I went to her, desperation
winning out over fear.

And though our years together
are mostly about what didn't work,
I cannot forget the plain white belt
she took from her dresser and slid
around my hips, adjusting a clean napkin
until it fit me exactly right,
and how she kissed me then, hard
in the middle of the forehead,
and explained how to soak
blood stains out in cold water.

JULIA KASDORF

First TV in a Mennonite Family

1968
The lid of the Chevy trunk couldn't close
on that wooden console with a jade screen
and gold flecks in the fabric over the speaker.

They sent us to bed then set it up
in the basement, as far from our rooms
and the dinner table as they could get,

out of sight for grandparents' visits.
The first morning, Mother studied the guide
and chose Captain Kangaroo for me,

but when we turned it on, the point of light
on the screen grew into black-and-white men
lifting a stretcher into the back of an ambulance.

Each click of the huge, plastic knob
flashed the same men, the same ambulance door
propped back like a broken wing.

After that we were forbidden to watch everything
except the Captain and "I Love Lucy."
Yet, when Dad returned from business in Chicago,

I heard him tell Mom how police beat the kids
under his hotel window, and I knew whatever it was,
that vague, distant war had finally come.

DOROTHY BARRESI

Vacation, 1969

Brothers rolling around in the big back seat,
all elbows and skirmishes,
complaints roared across Mt. Rushmore,
that hard family portrait,
across the Badlands purple with heat.
Back home, black children looted fire hydrants
under sinus-gray skies.
Our trailer was a cracker box ready to jackknife
when my sister, good reader,
practiced her phonetics: nā′päm.

I think it was just outside Turlock, California,
that I grew too sullen
for togetherness.
Rocking my new breasts in my arms,
I was conked out by hormones and Mick Jagger,
my face held in acne's blue siege.
So I pulled up oars early that August,
slept while the boys knocked heads
and my ironed-eyed parents took turns
lashed to the wheel,
America, by God, filling the car windows.

KATHRYN DANIELS

Big Sister Says, 1967

Beauty hurts, big sister says,
yanking a hank of my lanky hair
around black wire-mesh rollers
whose inside bristles prick my scalp
like so many pins. She says I'd better
sleep with them in.

She plucks, tweezes, glides razor
blades over tender armpit skin,
slathers downy legs with stinking
depilatory cream, presses straight lashes
bolt upright with a medieval-looking
padded metal clamp. *Looking good*

hurts, Beryl warns. *It's hard work*
when you're not born beautiful.

SUSAN FIRER

Basement Slow Dancing

Fear walks the world of the words
which pertain to our bodies.
–Pablo Neruda

I have forgotten whose basement it was,
but I remember blue electric
waterfall beer signs and an olive
green-musty sofa, and crepe-paper,
a 60's big-haired girl group on
the record player, and we were 13 & slow
dancing. (13, the best age to
slow dance: hardly anything precedes
the dance; certainly, nothing follows it.
It's all dance, an introduction
to the always from then on
mystery of the opposite.) We all were
like a field of yellow globe flowers
that always seem about to open,
but never do. All of us swayed
together in the basement dark,
in the night dark, in the dark
of our coming bodies and lives.
I didn't know what it was that
first time; I didn't even have a name
for it (that would come later
through jokes filled with pencils
and pockets). The important fact
is that all the words people taught me:
erection, hammer, hot rod, pole, hard-on,
boner, rock candy—all the words were wrong,
were too callous, too flippant, too steely
for that sweet nudging, that strange
insistent champagne christening ghost
floating into me and finding a ghost partner

voyager who walked out of me to meet it.
This was not movie love fireworks or waves.
This was older: pumpkins falling in on themselves,
black fields shooting up purple, yellow, and pink
colors on dark, fragrant nights. This was kissing
your parents' dead, white bones then eating
from them. How many things are
our bodies too dumb to name, but smart enough
to remember? Our bodies were dancing
in dark beer sign lit basements to music
that only our bodies understood. Our bodies
were clinging to each other, helping each
other grow toward where we all would.
Like spoons that fit the mouth so perfectly
you never want to take them out, we were
dancing, perfectly, feeding the bodies forever
forecasts of one and another.

JULIE KING

To Mary at Thirteen

You taught me to bake
cookies when I was ten,
to measure into the oversized
blue bowl, to squeeze
dough through my fingers.
Nothing since has matched
that smoothness, that aroma
of sugar, butter, real
vanilla, the combining
of ingredients that had stood
alone in tin canisters
or bottles, pure and neat,
into something sliding
over my tongue. Nothing
since has matched the strands
of red hair escaping
your barrette, clean sweat
on your freckled nose,
as you silently concentrated
on your task, rolling
that dough into perfect glossy
balls, placing them two
inches apart on greased
sheets, criss-crossing
with our old, yellow-handled
forks. Nothing since
has matched Bobby Sherman
singing on the phonograph,
flour floating in oven-
warmed air, and your hips
swaying in silky, slow circles.

LAURA STEARNS

Barn Swallows

Surrounded by birch trees and sugar maples,
ghosts of appaloosas nickering hay
and cows with milk-white eyes, that barn
rose off the slow, uneven hill
of my childhood—a cobwebbed house
inhabited by barn swallows, a family who sang
all their words. Skittering in and out
of two carved crescent moons, those birds
knew the ribs of rafters and corners
where whispered dreams lay still.

Neighbor boys took the Bunnell girl there—
her toothless grin as she ambled barefoot
up nails laddering a beam of pocketknifed wood.
Mother warned my sisters and me away,
but we wedged a wide circle on Sundays after church,
eager to exchange our pale pinks and patent leathers
for wind-dried jeans, mud boots from Montgomery Ward's.
Lured by the windvane's spinning, we splattered
plums onto gray wood split by rain.
When only the dark stains answered,

we pulled open the door and entered single file
through flourdust light, sifting the musk
of mildew and snagged hems of calico and gingham.
Dangling our legs from the loft, we spoke of skeleton keys
and the idiot boy who lived two pastures over
with his mother who always jumbled our names.
And the white light the Widow Cooper followed,
calling in her will o' wisp, telling us it vanished
ice cold into the floorboards
the morning we found her kneeling,
her flannel nightgown trailing the bare linoleum.

Someday, my older sister said, I will live
in a mansion, and she described butlers
toting biscuits, the crepe paper lanterns
strung beside a pool where shooting stars
glistened and fell. My little sister and I
nodded, twining a bracelet of straw.
When hunger came, we bit into bitter apples.
Twisted the stems to an alphabet of boys
bent over polished chrome and engines.

The birds have it right, my older sister said,
they can always go. We knew the secret places
she meant: Lapland, the mud-baked Congo, everywhere
Father's glossy *National Geographic* took him
night after night under the front room's dim glow.
When we stumbled into the night air,
there was a new order to everything,
dinner plates being carried from cupboards to counters,
the electric fence buzzing,
and the Bunnell girl lying on her bed, staring
at the bluebell wallpaper suddenly grown old.

DONNA HILBERT

The Pursuit of Knowledge

I learned about sex from Freud and Grace Metalious,
a few details and the will to know.
From *Interpretation of Dreams*,
I learned the word *libido*,
rolled it around my mouth like sour
lemon candy. On the days I ditched school
I smoked Camels and read over and over
the good parts of *Peyton Place*
now loose pages in my hands,
how Rodney Harrington reached for Helen's
bare hard breast,
not noticing the lights until she screamed,
the lights of the truck that changed everything,
that trailer truck barreling down
the highway toward them.

The Word Made Flesh

I looked up the words
but I could not find them.
I found *breast* and *menstruation*
and *period*—colorless words
for the bright smear on my pants,
the breath breathless in my mouth.
I could not find the real words
for my heart's desire,
for my body's breaking.
There were no words for his smell
or the taste of his sweaty skin
(Island beaches on my tongue)
in the *American Heritage Dictionary*
my parents gave me to ensure
my success in this new language.

I went to the Public Library
to the big fat dictionary,
the one that felt like his weight
on my lap, but I could not find
a word for the rocking on the daybed,
for his tongue like a fish in my mouth.
Only *foreplay* & *intercourse*,
only *privates puberty pudendum*.
None of these words spelled out
my secret I couldn't tell anyone.

I gave up trying to find
his body next to mine,
the small of his back in English.
And I paged through *El Pequeño*
Larousse Ilustrado,
hoping to come upon him
in my first, more heartfelt language,

the accents bearing down
on the sweetly musical syllables,
words rooted in love,
vowels stewing in juices.
But I did not know what to look for
in my deserted childhood Spanish
with Papi still turning the pages
to *la lengua castellana.*

There was no way to say
what I wanted, he wanted,
they did not want me to want,
no way to do it but do it,
lie down and slide my tongue
into his all-American mouth,
looking for the words to say
what was happening in silence
in my *cuerpo* and his heart,
in his *corazón* and my body.

from "Sound Bites"

KATHRYN DUNN

I wish I could tell you

there was a war; there wasn't. People died
of polio and disappeared from shame,
but no one had uniforms. Guns
were attitudes, words were ammunition;

girls were shot regularly. "Hey babe,
which way to the high school . . . ?"
Trick questions to establish age and degree
of willingness or fear.

Don't answer them, just don't answer.

My friends and I drank Colt 45 because
it was stronger. It froze in the woods,
we thawed it out. Hey babe, we took long walks
down side roads, short walks into town.

We stood in front of Goodnow Pearson's
department store, looked across the street
at Pete's Pool Room, next door to the place
where our 8th grade English teacher worked

weekends, dispatching taxis, smoking,
staring past us like we weren't even there
across from Pete's Pool Room, hey babe.
Our allies were younger boys who drank with us,

got us beer, wanted more, much more, but adjusted,
settled for coolness. Across from Pete's,
we watched the guys go in. "Old enough to bleed,"
they joked as they opened the door,

"old enough to breed," they chuckled.
We watched them, considered our fates.

RITA DOVE

Adolescence—I

In water-heavy nights behind grandmother's porch
We knelt in the tickling grasses and whispered:
Linda's face hung before us, pale as a pecan,
And it grew wise as she said:
    "A boy's lips are soft,
    As soft as baby's skin."
The air closed over her words.
A firefly whirred near my ear, and in the distance
I could hear streetlamps ping
Into miniature suns
Against a feathery sky.

Adolescence—II

Although it is night, I sit in the bathroom, waiting.
Sweat prickles behind my knees, the baby-breasts are alert.
Venetian blinds slice up the moon; the tiles quiver in pale
 strips.

Then they come, the three seal men with eyes as round
As dinner plates and eyelashes like sharpened tines.
They bring the scent of licorice. One sits in the washbowl,

One on the bathtub edge; one leans against the door.
"Can you feel it yet?" they whisper.
I don't know what to say, again. They chuckle,

Patting their sleek bodies with their hands.
"Well, maybe next time." And they rise,
Glittering like pools of ink under moonlight,

And vanish. I clutch at the ragged holes
They leave behind, here at the edge of darkness.
Night rests like a ball of fur on my tongue.

RITA DOVE

Adolescence—III

With Dad gone, Mom and I worked
The dusky rows of tomatoes.
As they glowed orange in sunlight
And rotted in shadow, I too
Grew orange and softer, swelling out
Starched cotton slips.

The texture of twilight made me think of
Lengths of Dotted Swiss. In my room
I wrapped scarred knees in dresses
That once went to big-band dances;
I baptized my earlobes with rosewater.
Along the window-sill, the lipstick stubs
Glittered in their steel shells.

Looking out at the rows of clay
And chicken manure, I dreamed how it would happen:
He would meet me by the blue spruce,
A carnation over his heart, saying,
"I have come for you, Madam;
I have loved you in my dreams."
At his touch, the scabs would fall away.
Over his shoulder, I see my father coming toward us:
He carries his tears in a bowl,
And blood hangs in the pine-soaked air.

LESLIE ADRIENNE MILLER

Warts

I grew a big one on my thumb. At first
an itchy blister with a white halo,
it clutched a pocket of seeds and intrigued me.
Though I'd seen them roughening the knees,
elbows, knuckles of boys, no girl I knew
had one. So I dug at the tiny fortress
at night till it broke through its first
ring, and scattered pods of dread
down the length of flesh below my thumb.
I was sure it meant I couldn't be loved.

By day, I peeled scraps from the top,
by night I gouged at the roots and left
a telltale spatter of picking in my sheets.
For months I tried to hide what I grew
in the dark garrison of my childhood,
asking for Band-Aids too often, complaining
of innocent encounters with stumps, stones,
cats and concrete, but the warts were something
else, unstoppable flowering of my own
wrong stigmata. I sobbed and dreamed
of the rusty shreds in their milky pockets,
wanted to believe I'd simply touched
one toad too many, but kids said toad pee
couldn't *really* do that.

So it was me. Maybe I'd touched myself
too much at night, exploring the strange
heat of my secret nest. I lay for hours
in the tub soaking them white, hoping
they'd drop like scales, hoping I'd become
immaculate and girl enough again. I held
my forefinger tight over the rotten place
on my thumb for all of a year before my mother

noticed and bought the burning liquid
that crackled when it hit the hard hearts
and stripped them to dry, harmless flakes of chalk.

But it was only the tops that came off
and I went to piano lessons ashamed,
holding my monster fingers over the dainty
keys for the teacher's punishing stick.
At last my mother took me, terrified, to the city
to a doctor who gassed my gnarled gardens
till they shriveled. But the roots held,
sprouted every year and joined the swell
of girlish worries: *Where are my promised*
breasts, my peaches and cream, my good blood?

I went on with piano lessons that never took,
cures and silent crushes that didn't either,
and all the time I knew it wasn't done
with me, whatever it was my body
was dredging up in the dark, the burrow
and flourish of armies of unthinkable things,
bones, sores and protrusions, my secret
fields where nothing fair, pure
or girl enough to be loved
could ever grow.

HARRIET LEVIN

Bird of Paradise

Orange and purple fanning outward
like the bandanna around the head
of my sister, a fevered span
traversed in the clink
of two glasses. She drinks gin from each,
pinning a skirt in the mirror,
measuring the distance,
the remorse, because
she is always coming back
as someone else.
We think she has come home to us,
bird of paradise, finally driven out
from her world of drugs and pain
where the ground slopes
unevenly, and no word is true enough
to follow mile after mile.
The night she came home
she called me outside
with a handful of stones
against my window,
her red hair aglow.
I watched as she staggered behind the garage,
holding her stomach,
rolling from side to side on the grass.
And each time we bend down
to lift her up
she hurts us,
her bruised arms,
unable to feel a thing,
fixed around my father's neck.

MARIE HOWE

The Boy

My older brother is walking down the sidewalk into the
suburban summer night:
white T-shirt, blue jeans—to the field at the end of the
street.

Hangers Hideout the boys called it, an undeveloped plot, a
pit overgrown
with weeds, some old furniture thrown down there,

and some metal hangers clinking in the trees like wind
chimes.
He's running away from home because our father wants to
cut his hair.

And in two more days our father will convince me to go to
him—you know
where he is—and talk to him: No reprisals. He promised. A
small parade of kids

in feet pajamas will accompany me, their voices like the first
peepers in spring.
And my brother will walk ahead of us home, and my father

will shave his head bald, and my brother will not speak to
anyone the next
month, not a word, not *pass the milk*, nothing.

What happened in our house taught my brothers how to
leave, how to walk
down a sidewalk without looking back.

I was the girl. What happened taught me to follow him,
whoever he was,
calling and calling his name.

MICHELE SPRING-MOORE

Adolescent Rag: Greece, New York, 1981

for Patrick, Shari, and T. J.

Get over it or die with it, we threw at those who scrutinized
us, young queers—gays, we called ourselves then—out
for an early breakfast, plunked down in booths of avocado
vinyl
at Perkins Family Restaurant after *Rocky Horror Picture
Show* had wound

up once again, or the bars had closed. Why did I suppose
suburbanites
spilling out of singles joints and straight nightclubs wouldn't
stare
at us? A gaggle of teenage girls and boys in tuxedo jackets,
white
makeup, garter belts, black fishnet stockings with gaping
tears

all over our thighs, would grab attention at a costume ball,
not to mention
the local pancake house. The star of our show, a nineteen-
year-old fag,
theatrically bent (he raised money for AIDS and flouted
convention
for the next decade as a rubber-breasted, well-heeled drag

queen), ordered hot fudge banana split sundaes and sucked
the life out of the plump unnaturally red maraschino
cherries
till some of our party giggled, flirted, blushed
and studly guys at tables with girlfriends or buddies

glared at him over steaming coffee. But his was the sorcery
of camp,

ours the safety of naïveté, beginners' luck, a more tolerant
time:
end of the Carter era, just before bashing fairies with
baseball bats
became acceptable, even praised. Legally, of course, it's
considered a crime

to kill us, but I brandish a file an inch thick with clippings,
ten
years of queers called names, beaten, knifed, murdered, and
I long
for those extinct days, remember nostalgically nights when
I thought it dreadful that someone dared *look* at us wrong.

Mad River

Two dollars and sixty-five cents
at the Hot Spot Take-Out Shack
for one chili dog and a coke,
Birmingham, Alabama, 1979.
I kissed a Greyhound bus driver
too many times so I could eat,
I got one chili dog, I wanted two,
thought I'd get two. Lucky I'm not dead.
I asked him about his children, his
fourteen-year-old daughter saved my life,
pulled up his rotten conscience like
regurgitation, black bile memory—I said
How old is your daughter, afraid he'd want
more for his money, and in the slant light
of his dark Chevy he saw a slice
of my young girl face and said,
She's fourteen, I better get you back
to the depot, and the black stench
of his twisted conscience wanted one more
kiss, one more kiss to get me back
to the bus station and my long ride home,
to wanting to spit up the dark beans,
their reddish bodies staining my insides
like a dead baby, like a blood spill,
my heart pumping its mad river with
sixty cents in my pocket and twenty-six
hours till home, I prayed for rain,
I prayed for morning.

LAURA KASISCHKE

Fatima

God exists. Instead
we are a group of teenage girls, drunk
at one of those awful
carnivals in a field, out
between the airport and the mall.
It's raining, and this
has become a festival
of mud, which is just
fine with us. A man

with hundreds of tattoos
has taken a fancy to Heidi
and is slipping her extra darts
to lob at the balloons. There are sirens
every time she misses, and she wins
nothing. Why

is there straw in the mud, why
is it plastered now to the wet
sleeves of our leather jackets? Something
cruises into the air
with its light bulbs zapping,
and when we turn around, the man

has disappeared with Heidi. Am I wrong
or has every teenage girl been
at this same carnival in the rain, in 19-
78, with four wild friends and a fifth of peach
schnapps in her purse with its bit
of rawhide fringe? Music

spins at us and away from us
as the Octopus starts up
its scrambling disco dance. Am I

the one who says *Don't worry*
she'll be back or have I
gone to the Port-o-Potty
to barf again by now? Imagine

hours later
when we are terrified and sober and
still waiting, when she
re-appears with her hand
tucked into the back
pocket of the tattooed man
who has no T-shirt on now under
his black vinyl vest
so we can see all
his swastikas and naked
ladies—imagine

that we are just
a few peasant girls
on a hill in Portugal. It's night, but the sun's

swung out of the sky
like a wrecking ball on fire
and even the skinny whores

in their ice-cold brothel smile
when the Fascists are gripped
with cramps
and shudder in their shiny
uniforms with tassles. Imagine
when we see Heidi:

her blurred blue robes
in the distance, her soft
virgin voice, and the way
it knocks us to our knees
like a crate of fruit, tossed
off a truck
and smashing into the street.

GERALDINE CONNOLLY

An Afternoon in the World

I remember how the nuns
spit it out, hissing—
the word "secular,"
as Rosie and I slithered
past school down the hill,
to the shopping mall
and gorged ourselves on candy,
hot chocolates, forbidden movies
among blazing marquees,
soft-lit, carpeted boutiques.

Escaping evening rosary
again, we descended
to North Hills Shopping Center
to rise on long, shining escalators
into a paradise of costume jewelry,
evening wear and perfume atomizers.
After days of the words "discipline"
and "spiritual," after the dry
prayers at breakfast, at lunch,
choir practice, piano practice,

forced study hall, hours
in chapel at Angelus, Vespers,
through squadrons of clerks
we hurried, into mountains
of stacked dry goods, draping
paisley shawls and strings of pearls
over our dull gray uniforms,
dabbing *Crepe de Chine,*
Shalimar, Orange Musk
onto our wrists, slipping
into sling-backed leather pumps

with stiletto heels, pulling
long silky nylons and garters up
over our secretly shaved legs.

Where are you now, Rosie,
and where are those fuzzy sweaters,
electroplated rings, that orange
yarn we bought and spooled
around our boyfriends' class rings
before we hung them
from our necks, that bright pink
polish we slathered over them
in a sticky heap, and the
lipstick with silver flecks that
tasted of rainwater? Where
are those tortoise shell compacts of blush,
the mascara wands? As if a wand
and a sweater could turn us
into models and not those
gray-blazered schoolgirls
in oxford shoes and high socks

running back up the road
with our paper sacks of merchandise,
running hard, having stayed
too long, rushing so as not to
miss supper, and holding
that taste of the secular
beneath our tongues
like those bright-colored
candy rings we favored,
lemon, watermelon, lime
and cherry, those lifesavers.

ALISON TOWNSEND

Smoke

I knew about your reputation
before I knew you, heard how you'd stagger—
drunk off your ass at a keg party—
into a car with the boys' basketball team
and go down on every one. I'd seen them
dump you off afterwards, shoving you
out the door with empty Budweiser bottles
and ash trays of Marlboro butts.

But I needed to know you
and you knew to reach for me,
and the night I stepped forward
when you stumbled and fell from the car
became the two of us laughing each day
over cigarettes in the girls' room
before the bell sent us running—
you to Voc Tech Cosmetology,
me to Honors French.

You sewed me an Indian print dress
drenched with sandalwood and patchouli.
We skipped out of school, hitchhiked,
ripped off mirror dresses and albums,
and danced together in the bathroom
at the Om coffee house, the faint blue smoke
of our first joints swirling around us like silk.

I thought we told one another everything.

But what I remember now
is how you begged me to sleep over,
even on school nights.
And how we lay beside one another
in your French Provincial beds,

listening to your father
walk back and forth outside your door.
I feel better when you're here, you said once,
sinking into sleep like a child
while I stared at your collection
of "Dolls from around the World"
and they stared back at me

the way they must have stared at him
when he came into your room
and put those hands that sliced
through sides of beef each day
upon you and made you do it.
Until you got it right. Until
it was what you knew how to do best.
Until there was no going back
from the boys in the car
or your job as a call girl in Denver.

And God forgive me, Amanda.
I never even tried to phone
or meet you for a drink
the way we used to meet
for cigarettes in the girls' room,
my hand on your cheek,
all the things never said
laid out on the table between us,
smoke still rising
through the bright blond
garden of your hair.

JILL BIALOSKY

Stairway to Heaven

My girlfriend and I snuck out
of our houses at midnight
on a Cleveland winter night
and met at the corner of our block.
Our mission was to find the two gas station
attendants we had spotted the night before.
We didn't know their names,
only their oily hands and dark coats.
Marie had big boobs and soft, Chek lips.
I was a quiet teenager with slight curves
and deep, skirting eyes.
We were a sensible team:
she was the target and I was the protection.
One boy was cuter than the other,
that's how it always went.
Marie would get in the back seat
and neck with the cute one
and I'd stay in front pressed against
the passenger door talking to the gawky driver
with a scar underneath his eye or bad teeth
above the sound of "Stairway to Heaven" or something
by Fleetwood Mac, until their lips in the back
were bruised and puffy.
Eventually, the driver pulled over
and let us out at the curb.
Marie scribbled her phone number on a matchbook.
For two or three days we'd linger near the phone
until pissed-off and pumped with revenge
we'd go out again, stalking the night
for the new replacements.
This time was my turn, I decided.
Outside the Sohio
we leaned against the unleaded
and waited for their shift to end.

When we got to the car
I slipped in the back,
ignoring Marie's tug on my sleeve.
The good one slipped in next.
The tape began: "Lucy in the Sky with Diamonds,"
joint lit, and within minutes
we were in the haze of music and drug
until we'd open the door
and let the cold blast of air rescue us.
His name was Randy.
The very minute the words slipped
from his lips I didn't want to forget him.
Randy, I thought, over and over
as he turned a lock of my hair
in his finger and began his work.
No, I *liked* the smell of petroleum
on his neck, his nicotine lips.
I could make him up in my mind
for weeks, I thought, without
knowing a single thing about him.
This time we'd wait by my phone
and when it rang I'd say, Randy,
Hello. Two words.
And the long dark dialogue
would begin.

4
The Music of the Rest of Our Lives

SILVIA CURBELO

Janis Joplin

There is a song like a light
coming on too fast, the eyes
blink back the static of the road
and in the distance you can almost see
the clean, sweet glow of electric guitars.

Call it the music of the rest of our lives,
a stranger's face peering through
a window, except that face is yours,
and mine. Music like backtalk,

like wind across your heart,
cigarette smoke and bourbon.
Music our mothers must have held
softly between damp sheets
before taxes, before layoffs,
before the first door closing.

Not piano lessons, not a hymn
or a prayer, or a soft voice
singing you to sleep, but a song
like a green light on summer evenings
after a ball game, after rain,
when the fields finally let themselves go,
and we'd drive past the Westinghouse plant,
past Vail and Arcadia. Music
of never going back.

I'm talking about car radios,
about backseats and hope,
and the jukebox at Pokey's
where the local boys tried
their new luck on anyone
and the real history of the world

was going down, nickels and
dimes, the music floating
at the far end of a first kiss,

the first light of the body
that isn't love but is stronger than love,
because it must not end,
because it never lasts.

JUDITH HOUGEN

Points of No Return

This is the year Elvis dies and Delavan, Wisconsin, finally
gets a Pizza Hut and I'm working another summer
  scooping up
ice cream at Lake Lawn Lodge just before my senior year.

I scratch out rhymes on the back of placemats between
  customers
and on a half hour break write my first bad poem about loss.
My mother packs me dinners, making sure one of my
  two aprons

is clean, though inevitably faint stains map the cloth
like the outlines of ghostly continents. I can throw together
five banana splits without blinking. The trick is to peel

and slice the fruit before you flip in ice cream. It'll melt
less. That table tipped me a dollar for the effort. It's a slow
  August
afternoon and Marge, the cashier, announces Elvis is dead

in a voice that sounds so monumental I'm surprised I feel
nothing. Within days, the number of roadside velvet
  painting
concessions shoots up like weeds with different Elvis poses,

varying sneers. I want to write a poem about it: *each one*
a billboard for death and *middle-aged women maundering*
(my new word) *among the portraits like headstones.* This is

the year I dream about college in Minneapolis, loving
and hating Delavan, Wisconsin, the way every kid loves and
  hates
a small town they are about to outgrow, not knowing what
  to term

the ambivalence, not understanding the signs, how points
of no
return are so effortless you can't mark them until after
the door
is shut. The ice cream parlor closes at ten and I mop up
counters,

gray dishrag coaxing chrome spigots to shine before it all
starts again. I think about Elvis occasionally since Marge
is in mourning and about the hysterical fans run over at
his funeral.

In seventeen years, I have never known a desperate passion
that makes you leave yourself like that. I report for work
six days
a week, keep my uniform clean, tolerate tourists from
Chicago.

But it is all the edge of something, some place I need to go
mapped
out on the poem folded in my apron pocket, ticket to a
destination
I can't even picture, a new way to see this simple, endless
field of my life.

KIM ADDONIZIO

Them

That summer they had cars, soft roofs crumpling
over the back seats. Soft, too, the delicate fuzz
on their upper lips and the napes of their necks,
their uneven breath, their tongues tasting
of toothpaste. We stole the liquor
glowing in our parents' cabinets, poured it
over the cool cubes of ice with their hollows
at each end, as though a thumb had pressed
into them. The boys rose, dripping, from long
blue pools, the water slick on their backs
and bellies, a sugary glaze; they sat easily on high
lifeguard chairs, eyes hidden by shades,
or came up behind us to grab the fat we hated
around our waists. For us it was the chaos
of makeup on a bureau, the clothes we tried on
and on, the bras they unhooked, pushed
up, and when they moved their hard
hidden cocks against us we were always
princesses, our legs locked. By then we knew
they would come, climb the tower, slay anything
to get to us. We knew we had what they wanted:
the breasts, the thighs, the damp hairs pressed flat
under our panties. All they asked is that we let them
take it. They would draw it out of us like
sticky taffy, thinner and thinner until it snapped
and they had it. And we would grow up
with that lack, until we learned how to
name it, how to look in their eyes and see nothing
we had not given them; and we could still
have it, we could reach right down into their
bodies and steal it back.

Lawn Ornaments

The first time I stood in the charged air
of female rage, I didn't know that night
would always have something to do with it,
that if anyone ever kissed you so your blood
lurched into your throat and your new body
leaked and burned, and then tried to pretend
it never happened, you'd have to get them
back. That's what must have happened to Alice
and why she needed seven girls
in someone's father's finned Buick
careening through the spring night
like the gray weight of a mother possum,
babies packed away in her pockets.

At first we meant only to filch a few
pink flamingos and dump them in his yard.
Whatever the boy had done, we didn't need
to know. We let her anger lead us, choose one
of our names each time we'd circled
the block enough to be sure the take
was right: terribly grinning elves,
a whole family of tactless yellow ducks,
plastic pinwheels that would snap
and hiss with a little wind.
We couldn't tell from the street
how heavy they were, how many girls
it would take to carry the hunched
and crude creature that turned out
to be a plaster lamb. And we didn't
anticipate the mealy bugs, the wet worms
that clung to its underside, dropped
through the gaps in our blouses
as we ran screeching to the car. Alice
drove, welcomed us each back into the musty

interior of the Buick now filling with
drying dirt, grass clippings and edges
of molded plastic sharp as her own
laughter at the boy's dark house,
a street where no lawn ornament
ever winked an exaggerated eye.

It isn't over yet, our imperviousness
to adult pain, but we can taste the fakeness
of it like the smell of wet plastic
in the car, chewed baby toys, dolls left out
overnight so their skin fades and stinks.
Alice's rage has filled our laps,
our ears, and we are laughing back, someone
has even peed her pants a little because
the curved neck of a pink flamingo has snapped
in the wind of our flight. She dangles
the wet bulb over the seat like a puppet,
the head of the boy we're helping Alice kill.

We're jammed so tight among the mushrooms,
leprechauns and giant spiky flowers
underfoot, that we crush and crack the ducks,
fling out cartoon daisies, dump the swollen
lady bug with stupid surprised eyes.
We tangle the flamingos by their awful
hooked necks and pour all the dented
characters of our childhood stories
into the yard of the boy we can't
really hurt.

When you're a girl, rage and shame
have the same sinister, too-bright smile,
and that perfectly shaved blue hill
is the body of all the men who will
make you feel it. You'll have to run
across that moonless expanse in secret
and at night; you'll have to be armed
with laughter, and girls who'll help you

make that yard crazy with cuteness,
girls who'll fill the smashed grin
of the garden dwarf with someone's tube
of Poppy Pink and jam him upside down
in a bed of plastic roses.

PAMELA GEMIN

Senior Picture, 1971

I take it all back,
each dirty, lowdown thing I ever said
and felt and thought about you, honey,
and all I put you through.

I take back your Clearasil zits and Midol cramps,
take back those cheap 4-inch gold-plated hoops
that infected your earlobes
and snagged your silk shirts;
I take it all back to the K-Mart for you,
stand in the returns line
with armfuls of too-tight bras, blue eyeshadows,
Uncurl and water weight pills.

I take back the menthol stink of those nasty
fags you smoked, breathe in the foul clouds
you blew out your bedroom window;
take out the butts you double-wrapped
in Kleenex, sprayed with Glade,
snuck out to the backyard trash can;

take back the pink frosted lipstick
and jasmine cologne you stole from Hudson's;
take back the drive-in nights
you puked popcorn and apple wine
out the windows of fast-moving cars;
take back your dancing wild at the Bowl-O-Drome;

your animal, rabid fear of touching
and being touched; your fear of boylust burning
bright as a thousand votives
in St. Joseph's vestibule;
fear of the Lone Airborne Sperm,
fear of the Lord's cool hand

set down hard upon your backside,
fear of His crown of thorns
set down hard upon your hairdo;
take back your venial sins chalked up in fives
on your blank slate soul.

I take back your fear of fat, stronger
than your fear of God, the fear
that kept saying *no thank you,*
no thank you, none for me, please;

that whittled you down and down
with your chocolate milk lunches
from 116 to 106 to 96 pounds
that Easter you went to Florida;

and even with studio-tinted cheeks
and hair the photographer made too red,
naturally wavy hair set straight
on juice cans and Dippity-Do the night before;
and even in spite of that goofy far-off someday look
the picture pulled out of your face
from God knows where,

I can see it so crystal
clearly now, decades too late,
see your momma was all along right
about you;
you were one sweet bird,
one inside/outside beautiful
special girl.

ALISON STONE

Rocket to Russia

I woke up with purple hair and Paul
Beside me grinning as he tried
To put a blue stripe on Jenni.
She rolled over, stained
The pillowcase. My contact lenses
Felt like glass, mouth tasted
Of socks. I had to get to school. We were doing
One of the important wars.

Walking to the subway in rain I cursed Mom
For lending me her pointy boots. Jenni and I
Discussed Shakespeare and mescaline, and why
Our boyfriends preferred men. Krazy Kolor ran,
staining my forehead purple-blue. On the train
A woman asked if I'd been mugged.

RITA RANDAZZO

The Sixties

I remember them,
which proves I didn't
fully participate.

I didn't see Janis and Jimi
in San Francisco like my
best friend from high school,
but did send her money
when she wrote she was
eating from garbage cans.

I never dropped a tab of acid
or wallowed in a group grope,
just smoked a little pot
and sliced off the TV antenna
playing stoned fencing.

I wasn't beat up in Chicago
in '68, I merely got married.

Mild stuff, not worthy
of that legendary decade:
marriage and other
old friendships,
the occasional grass
and high spirits.

I came of age in
the eye of a hurricane,
wearing white gloves,
riding the subway home.

CATHY SONG

Sunworshippers

"Look how they love themselves,"
my mother would lecture as we drove through
the ironwoods, the park on one side,
the beach on the other, where sunworshippers,
splayed on towels, appeared sacrificial,
bodies glazed and glistening like raw fish in the market.
There was folly and irreverence to such exposure,
something only people with dirty feet did.
Who will marry you
if your skin is sunbaked and dried up like beef jerky?
We put on our hats and gloves
whenever we went for a drive.
When the sun broke through the clouds,
my mother sprouted her umbrella.
The body is a temple we worship
secretly in the traveling revivalist tent of our clothes.
The body, hidden, banished to acceptable
rooms of the house, had only a mouth
for eating and a hole for eliminating
what the body rejected: the lower forms of life.
Caramel-colored stools, coiled heavily
like a sleeping python, were a sign
we were living right.
But to erect a statue of the body
and how the body, insolent and defiant
in a bikini, looked was self-indulgent, sun-
worshipping, fad diets and weight-lifting proof
you loved yourself too much.
We were not allowed to love ourselves too much.
So I ate less, and less, and less,
nibbling my way out of meals—
the less I ate, the less
there was of me to love.
I liked it best when standing before the mirror,

I seemed to be disappearing into myself,
breasts sunken into the cavity of my bird-cage chest,
air my true element which fed
in those days of college, snow and brick bound,
the coal fire in my eyes.
No one knew how I truly felt about myself.
Fueled by my own impending disappearance,
I neither slept nor ate, but devoured radiance,
essential as chlorophyll,
the apple's heated core.
Undetected, I slipped in and out of books,
passages of music, brightly painted rooms
where, woven into the signature of voluptuous vines,
was the one who flew one day out the window,
leaving behind an arrangement of cakes and ornamental
  flowers;
to weave one's self, one's breath, ropes of it, whole
and fully formed, was a way of shining
out of this world.

KATHRYN DUNN

The first time I almost made love

was with you in a motel
over by the liquor store
and the Medi-Mart Mall.

Later, when I looked in the mirror,
my face was a rich deep color
I'd never seen before, and my hair
looked like the women in the magazines.

It was in that moment of sudden beauty
that I understood: the next time
a man made me feel that way

he would own me. That's when
you lost me, not two years later
when I packed my records and books,

asked you to mail them to me;
not when you drank too much
and wrecked the apartment, not even
when the boxes never came.

ALLISON JOSEPH

The First Time

Old wives' tales didn't help,
locker room advice didn't prepare me
to be both broken and whole,

molten and arid, each cell in my body
not knowing whether to weep
or celebrate, whether to pull you in,

push you away. Was this the sort of peril
women were meant for, this inexplicable
danger? Eyes closed, I can go back

to that single precarious moment
when you separated me from myself, broke
the passage open, pushing past my ache,

past the gasp that rose from me
when you entered, making room,
settling in as if you belonged.

Afraid to move, afraid not
to move, I wanted distractions—
your mouth on mine, your hands

on my breasts. But you thrust deeper,
held my back tight with both hands
as we rocked in pain and sweetness,

and I felt old, older as I realized
there was no easy satisfaction
in this, no simple union

or sudden comfort, only greater questions,
only a bond we made looser each time
we sunk to our knees, every time I let you in.

DENISE DUHAMEL

Ragweed

The first night I stayed at my reluctant boyfriend's
apartment,
I promised him I'd be no trouble. He didn't want me leaving
a toothbrush or tee shirt. He liked it best when we had our
clumsy sex
at my place, before midnight, so he could catch the last train
to Revere. The T was full of sandals and coolers after our
date.
I promised at that summer's end I'd be out before breakfast
the next day. I fell asleep looking at the ceiling,
his clammy back to my left, the open window above my
head.
I tried to pretend that I was in Southern France
but was distracted by the squabbling neighbors, by dragging
mufflers.
The ocean's lullaby was a whole two blocks away,
and besides, the beach was littered with filth.
When I woke up, my eyelids refused to part, like dream
within dream.
I checked to make sure I could move my arms and legs
before I tapped a panicked tap somewhere along my
boyfriend's arm.
He screamed, thinking he was dreaming too when he saw
my face,
big and red, not at all as it looked the night before. I cried
and the tears loosened my lids so I could get up and see
myself
in the mirror. My cheeks puffed up like two pregnant bellies.
My eyes were barely visible through the slits. I reached
for my inhaler, not sure if my asthma was part of the
swelling.
My boyfriend called an ambulance, saying he didn't have the
money

to pay for it. I remember trying to make a joke, that Emily Post
says men aren't responsible for any medical expenses
women may incur on a date, especially when the pattern
has been dutch treat. He didn't laugh, he didn't want
to go to the hospital. He was sure my desire to spend the day with him
was so great that I ballooned my own face. In the emergency room,
the doctors thought it was kidney failure until I explained
my peeing schedule. They ran a series of tests
as my boyfriend watched *Tom and Jerry* in the waiting room,
sugar from his powdered donut dusting his tapping foot.
The doctors finally said I had a severe allergic reaction,
one so rare it could have been written up in medical journals.
My face wouldn't shrink back to normal for four to six days.
I rode the subway back to Boston alone. Through my blurry vision
I could see children staring as I rattled the bottle of antihistamines
in my pocket. I tripped over Boston's cobblestones
and a few teenagers laughed, as they would at a retarded person.
My cheeks were hot when I touched them.
My roommates thought I'd been beaten.
Funny that a field of ragweed could grow so near the ocean.
Funny that I had no desire to escape through his open window.
I called my boyfriend to tell him I'd arrived home safely.
He said to call him back when I looked normal again.

CATHLEEN CALBERT

My Mother Taught Me How to Be Poor,

all the little things, like thrift-shopping,
holding out dresses in front of my sister,
shouting, "Two dollars! A dollar-fifty!"
My sister preferred to spend her time

making things up about our family history:
dancing lessons, *Auhnt*, not *Ant*, Ginny.
She never understood how we could be
proud of paying so little for anything.

She'd go into banking, making her way
up from secretary to VP of Sales, pulling
in a bundle in the eighties, buying ninety-
dollar iced-tea pitchers, until everything

collapsed under the weight of a half-million-
dollar house and corporate downsizing.
She has little left except lots of pastel
furniture, closetfuls of costly clothes.

I have seen the rows of four-inch heels
she wore when she was thin and rich.
In her forties, she stands at a cashier
window all day, and they no longer fit.

She was my father's child: extravagant,
tacky, believing she was buying quality.
My mother's baby, I made sure I stayed
in school, thus never acquiring anything,

no color TV, VCR, answering machine,
my cars old Bugs beginning or ending
their second or third incarnations, beds
two-inch foam pads, the boards and bricks

for the books set up in each room I rented
in each shared household, sometimes full
of friendly girls, sometimes drugsellers,
or, briefly, sexual deviants and thieves.

I thumbtacked Maxfield Parrish posters,
as if I lived a life of sensuous beauty.
I learned to value time over money,
time to write, time to think, time to brood

over life's unfairness and my lack of money.
I learned how to walk, I learned bus routes,
to buy expensive smaller sizes of things since
I could never carry anything called "economy,"

to marry for love, not money, because, as she
said men, the bastards, the sons of bitches,
you've got to love them, and how to spend
half a weekly paycheck on Friday evening,

buying special packaged treats that we
wouldn't be able to have for another week
as we went back to living on rice and beans,
not expecting much but wanting everything.

LORI HORVITZ

Father's Advice

You're too lonely, that's why you can't sleep at night. You're out of touch with the world. You need to watch television. Why don't you join a synagogue?

Why are you always running off to Europe? What are you running away from? Why don't you visit Epcot Village, you'd love it. You don't need to run around Mexico shitting all day long.

Get out of your room and stop pulling on yourself. Run around the block a few times. Of course you have cavities, you eat candy from morning till night.

Invite a friend when you drive a long ways, you need someone to talk to. Ask the man if there's enough oil in the car. Don't let anyone in the car. If you crash, they'll sue the kishkas out of you.

Why don't you become a speech pathologist, it's good money and you don't have to work too hard. You should be making eighty thousand a year by now—just get a job in a bank, join the army, take the postal clerk test, become a psychiatric nurse, open up a Carvel.

You don't need to be reading Marx. He was a filthy bastard who never took a bath. Don't work too hard on your papers for school, just copy from the book and write "Ibid."

When are you gonna finish your degree already? Just write three odes and call it a day. Better yet, write something like Beowulf. People will think you're a genius.

Send grandma a recent photo of yourself. She wants to set you up with a police sergeant. He's Jewish. Why don't you find someone already? Get married and get it over with.

KELLY SIEVERS

Rochester, Minnesota, 1965

Hot tunnels wound beneath the ground,
hospital to dormitory to chapel. But we

chose to run through icy
air. With stiff white wings pinned

to our heads, we hugged our breasts
and flew. From women draped

in long folds of white we learned
to pull back blankets, expose one

arm, one leg, to bathe
the sick. *Here is the heart,*

Sister Ruth said, showing us empty
chambers, valves held tight

on tiny strings. *And the eye,*
one big black cow's eye,

its crystalline vitreous
hidden. Beneath the light from

three story windows we sat on gallery
benches to watch silent men

open the brain. At night
we dipped our fingers

in holy water then slid
into our single beds,

hiding our hot
and steaming hearts.

KIM ADDONIZIO

The Philosopher's Club

After class Thursday nights
the students meet at the Philosopher's Club.
It's right around the corner from the streetcar tracks
at the West Portal tunnel. No one bothers
to check I.D.s. Five or six of them
get shooters and talk—about sex, usually.
Let me tell you about this dildo I bought,
one girl says. She describes how it looks
when all the gadgets attached to it are going at once.
My girlfriend is pregnant, says one of the boys.
That's nothing, says another, I've got twins
I've never seen. It goes on like this all semester.
Gradually they learn each other's stories:
the girl raped at knifepoint in Florida,
the kid whose old man shot seven people
in a trailer park outside Detroit.
Life is weird, they agree, touching glasses.
The bartender flips channels on the TV,
the sound turned down.
Spoiled brats, he thinks. He imagines a woman
with the blonde's legs, the brunette's tits.
"Dynasty" looks boring and he quits
at a black-and-white newsreel about the Nazi camps—
piles of heads with their mouths open,
bodies with arms like chicken wings. On the jukebox
Otis Redding sings "Try a Little Tenderness."
One of the regulars stands there
popping his gum, jamming in selections.
The students, smashed, are hugging each other.
I love you, they all say. Outside, in the rain,
people are boarding a lit streetcar.
As it jolts toward the tunnel

some of them look back at the bar,
its staticky neon sign
the last thing they see as they enter the dark.

PAMELA GEMIN

When Van Morrison Sang

"Tupelo Honey,"
wouldn't we all turn to satin inside,
we girls playing euchre
and smoking and tossing back
lipsticked longnecks, hips rocking
out of our chairs
those Friday nights at Donna's?

She was already divorced by then,
but weren't we all still such believers;
didn't we close our eyes
and scream Jesus, I *love* this song,
even with Donna's heart
pounded flat, chicken-fried and forked up
on a Melmac platter; oh

hadn't we been through that blender
one speed or another;
hadn't we lived to tell
it again, threading it in
and out of Friday nights when Van
went down the hatch
all ginger smoke and sweetness?

And yes, we all wanted good jobs
for fair money, and cars
that would make it home,
and each other's lifetime love,
but sometimes, if only for Friday night,
didn't we just want to be
that girl

Van Morrison sang about,
that "angel of the first degree,"

who could ruffle her wings,
pass her glittering wand
over Van and his kind,
and make such music,
make a man sing like that?

MARIANNE BORUCH

The Vietnam Birthday Lottery, 1970

Not winter still, but not
quite spring, and any hope narrowed
to the dorm's TV
in the lounge downstairs, the official
gravel of its voice. And girls
in scattered chairs, not languid or wise-ass for once,
not distracted. Such a little screen: black
and white, and men who moved only
their mouths, in suits that made them
bigger. But the girls kept track,
and each had a birthday
hidden in that quiet like a flame
you'd cup a hand around,
in wind. The wind
was history and its filthy sweep, whatever
rots like that, in one head
or a thousand. On this day, all days
turned a tragic swift ballet. And thinking as I did
no *what if*, no boyfriend, nothing
staked directly in the heart to stay
and stay, I thought merely
a kind of cloud
filled the room, or smoke. You could see it
and smell it: everyone dark-dreaming there alone
though—what?—twenty, thirty of us?
The only light
was dread, one small window of it, with its
vacant men on the other side
poised above the spinning box like those
cheap quiz shows, and you could get
a gleaming washer or a spiffy car, an Oldsmobile
with any luck. Of course
you could. Of course, sobbed my friend
whose boy was suddenly born all wrong,

right on target, though, that moment, illegal
as an angel, already half
stupefied by visions
on a fake i.d. in some bar downtown. The whole
night like that: sobbing
or relief, dead drunk either way.
I fell asleep late to the boys'
roaring home, broken
wayward lines of them, the marked
and the saved, by moonlight or streetlight.
I can't remember which.

DORIANNE LAUX

Fast Gas

for Richard

Before the days of self service,
when you never had to pump your own gas,
I was the one who did it for you, the girl
who stepped out at the sound of a bell
with a blue rag in my hand, my hair pulled back
in a straight, unlovely ponytail.
This was before automatic shut-offs
and vapor seals, and once, while filling a tank,
I hit a bubble of trapped air and the gas
backed up, came arcing out of the hole
in a bright gold wave and soaked me—face, breasts,
belly and legs. And I had to hurry
back to the booth, the small employee bathroom
with the broken lock, to change my uniform,
peel the gas-soaked cloth from my skin
and wash myself in the sink.
Light-headed, scrubbed raw, I felt
pure and amazed—the way the amber gas
glazed my flesh, the searing,
subterranean pain of it, how my skin
shimmered and ached, glowed
like rainbowed oil on the pavement.
I was twenty. In a few weeks I would fall,
for the first time, in love, that man waiting
patiently in my future like a red leaf
on the sidewalk, the kind of beauty
that asks to be noticed. How was I to know
it would begin this way: every cell of my body
burning with a dangerous beauty, the air around me
a nimbus of light that would carry me
through the days, how when he found me,

weeks later, he would find me like that,
an ordinary woman who could rise
in flame, all he would have to do
is come close and touch me.

KATE GLEASON

In Winter Something inside Me Returns as to a Dark God

I love his scent of must,
so all-encompassing:
smoke in flannel, cloves
in mulled wine, love how
his breath on the night window
makes a shivery pattern
like a salt-fed, unlockable sea,
love how he dances me
in the crook of his arm.

I love how he is what
was missing from the light
and grateful dance
in the combed summer fields,
love the power he unleashes in me,
how I feel it, like a woman,
in my lower center
of gravity, the compressed deep
of an imploded star
that pulls into itself now.

I love how the pomegranate spills
its dark Milky Way
until I lose all train of thought
and am past any point
of return. I love his loneliness,
his ache for words, love
how he needs my mouth,
how he is everything
my mother warned me about.
Only more.

REBECCA McCLANAHAN

Bridal Rites

I sniff for hot coals, search
the sweaty firelit circle of women.
Around me they huddle, dimpled knees
pressed together to balance
Bride-Bingo cards. Stockings rub;
nylon heat rises. *B-7*, she shouts,
clacking dentures, and a murmur
like dishwater bubbles through the crowd.
Mother's cousin has won again,
two packages of colored clothespins.

I come barefoot to this passage,
hunting the one-eyed medicine woman
to lead me through the bloody breaking.
I want to ask how it feels.
Do you open like a tent flap?
Rough, his tongue, like a cat's on your skin?
Smooth? Do you slide together?
Where do his eyes go?
Do you remember? His scent,
does it stay in your hair?

They smile and bring me what they know:
yellow peignoir with uplift bra, Vegematic,
Tupperware. They caution me on leftovers,
how vital to keep the celery crisp.
We move to the table, where cashews
bed down with pastel mints. In the punchbowl,
dollops of sherbet float like breasts set free.
The women cut the cake into uniform slices.
Giggle. Snap my picture.
I leave heavy with their gifts,
watching for signs: the ancient moon,
the she-wolf howling.

RACHEL LODEN

Marrying the Stranger

Marrying the stranger
is like getting lost

on purpose

in the small
epiphanies
of the grass

the way it grows
in spring
so willing
to be green

lying beside him
like a drenched rose
in the rain
you ask only
to be forgotten

to be cast aside again

to change your way of dying
to steal out of your name

to marry
into the unknown

and in that ceremony
fatherless
to give yourself away

MAUREEN SEATON

The Contract / 1968

His towels
grace the floor.
I run a bath, his brown hair
floats to the top.
I step in puddles, wonder
where to place the blame.
My mother says, "That's
a man for you."
I'm outraged.
There are other atrocities.
"Calm down,"
my parents say,
taking his side.

I am Rosemary
in *Rosemary's Baby*
alone in a phonebooth,
out of dimes.
He looks so sane
in his crisp ironed shirt.
My parents seem so sure.
"You're his wife,"
my father says,
"What did you expect?"
I'm 20 years old,
I whisper. Somebody
help me.

SILVIA CURBELO

First Snow

for Laura (1954–1986)

In this car years ago. In this
old town. Weeds choking in the fields.
A sky like nothing I've seen. *Close
your eyes.* Every street a new
language. The land empty, land of
birds disappeared, even the sparrows.
Every porchlight on Maple Street
still burns for you. I'm wearing
my new coat with silver buttons that
throw little specks of light on
the dashboard. I'm hunched over
the car radio, your sister flipping
through the dial looking for the next
song, for the next window facing west.
In another month she will outgrow you.
I'm 17, I'm falling through the cracks
of myself. The world as we know it.
The first snow of the year.
We drive past Spain's store and past
the high school sliding all over
the road. We turn off 1st Street
and down Twit's hill with the brakes
locked and your sister cuts the lights.
I can hear you laughing.
Your long hair blows across my face
in perfect strands, beautiful
as a loom, the one thing
I want to remember.
Football banners are still tied
to car antennas. Once a year
the Tigers play the Knights.
We're running down the street

making ourselves small to fool
the wind. It's snowing hard.
Down at the Main Tap the boys
notice you first. Your hair falling
in wet strands down your face,
covering your eyes. Every night
a vast landscape. A love song
blowing out the jukebox on somebody
else's coin. So slow. You can almost dance.
It's warm inside but I'm keeping my coat on
on account of the buttons. A row
of orange lights flashes on and off
in the back over the Budweiser sign.
It's the end of October and every
sad pumpkin in the world wears a grin.
Even a fool could close his eyes
and pull a wish out of thin air.
I bum a cigarette from the first
fool that smiles at you and I
take it outside. The snow falling
all over that Ford Galaxy
makes me want to drive forever.
A drunk out in the parking lot
is singing Blue Moon.
Not one star in that sky.

KYOKO MORI

On the Edge of the Field

for Beth

I

You knew it wasn't love but spring and grief
and our mothers' suicides. He'd been married
a year to a girl at school. On weekends

he and I drove to the flat, still-brown
fields outside the city. We photographed
every mile of that landscape as though we

expected our mothers to appear
on the edge of the field, a grey blur that would
always turn out to be a tree stump

or a rock dug out and removed
to the side. We'd go back to his father's house
shut up till Easter and spend the night

locked into each other's restlessness. You
didn't ask or judge. You let me sleep in your
room late spring when he called and called,

I had nothing to say, no more grief to share.

II

The day before Easter, we walked the mile
to Stop and Go and carried home three
cartons of eggs to color. The lawn stretched

brown between the campus and the road. In
our hands, the thirty-six eggs were perfect white
worlds, a golden planet spinning inside

each. Later, the night you were drunk
after a dance and kept kissing me
on the mouth in front of the dorm, I should

have thought of them. *I wish you were a boy,*
you said. *I love you more than*
anyone. Each kiss, I should have known, was

a white egg you were handing me whole
and fragile cupped in your palm. I could have
opened my mouth to swallow that perfection,

but I turned and ran. Jagged breaths streamed
out instead of words—small ghosts I was
following or chasing, away from you.

III

This April, it's the same slow spring, so brown
and grey I scarcely notice the dark
flowering of maples. No one knows where you are

alive or dead. Driving the hundred miles
between my house and Milwaukee, I wish
I could connect the years of my life

as simply as one mile follows another
then another from Sheboygan to Port
Washington to Milwaukee so all the brown

fields that look the same are embraced into
the same journey. As it is, too many things
remain standing on the edge, not completely

in or out of the picture. Some days, I
imagine how it must be for you, remembering
me: a girl running away from your love

and turning into stone in the grey
distance. Nothing can move me in or out.
Meanwhile, I drive off the highway in

Fox Point to see the Lake cut up into
wedges of dark and light blues, some green,
by the lay of land under water. The knife

edge of light moves slow and patient over
water, scanning for marks of love.

5
Above the Chains of Flesh and Time

DONNA MASINI

Claim

Finally I just go down to bossa nova by the river
my father in my legs and all the city breathing.
The silver arm of the Williamsburg Bridge links me to
  Brooklyn. My beginnings.
I pushed through the groins of dancing people who dipped
  and spun
groaned under each other. The dim lights over the hi-fi,
the language of belly and bone,
a child spasmodically rocking a crib across the floor
one wall to the other,
the crucifix, the tilted landscapes
black slip on the doorknob *cha cha cha.*
Where failure was as easy to catch as measles I filled pages
  with the letter *I*—
the long bar linking sky and earth.
I dreamed prairies, decimals, blue horses, universities.
Over the tailfins of a black '58 Chrysler riding over the BQE
I saw a neon BRUNO hanging in the sky.
My father's name—spread beneath the moon, across the sky.
By the knees of the bridge the river spins and stirs.
I broke loose, headed east to glitter and coast,
attached myself to this, to that,
                    and end up at the river
grapevining the sidewalk, following the crossed bars,
leading the city with my hip,
smokestacks like trumpet valves
playing the boundary between failure and grace.

elaine

in the photographs
you're tan and slim
only the latest
tiny bikini to show
your perfect pared
down curves. For
days you'd eat ice
to squeeze into
the you you wanted.
I was afraid to
slither thru the
room, your tongue
a whip. My cheeks
stung where you
slapped with a
scowl that summer
at Champlain where
I longed for your
straight black hair.
Even your mother
toed the line when
you ranted in the
middle of supper,
would leap up to iron
some little white
pique shorts you
might need. Your
sister never had
such white teeth. I
hated you but dreamed
of being as thin.
You even bossed
the flowers. As
queen of four sons you

must have reigned,
married of course
to a doctor. When I
heard they'd sliced
the second sweet
breast away that
pressed like a nose
up in the air
into pale cotton,
I couldn't believe
anything of yours
could have grown
that far from
your control

JULIA KASDORF

After the Second Miscarriage

for Ellen

There are no guarantees in marrying doctors
or men who'd make suitable fathers.
I tell you, it has nothing to do with us
whether babies stay or slink out,
bloody lumps in the toilet, in the swirl
of the flush. Remember that summer,
the night we dropped our panties
like pale rinds on the sand
and swam out into that black lake, blameless
under those million Michigan stars.
We were so young then,
my body not yet parted by a man,
yours, barely smarting from the fetus
that was sucked from its womb. Think
how it was then, not to feel stones
under foot, our strong arms skimming
the water like loons.

CATHY SONG

Eat

My mother is holding my infant son
so I can eat the mustard cabbage
she has sweetened with brown sugar.
For the starving children in China,
I have learned to eat whatever I am given.
Even mustard cabbage, which I hate.
She nods approvingly.
Now I must eat to feed
not only all the world's starving children
but my own flesh and blood,
my infant son,
who fattens daily on my milk,
my milk that trickles a thin blue stream
into his wet pink mouth.

I grow thinner.

He is sucking the living
daylights out of you,
says my mother,
and with a bamboo rice stick paddle,
she slaps another helping onto my plate.

Rainy Dawn

I can still close my eyes and open them four floors up
looking south and west from the hospital, the approximate
direction of Acoma, and farther on to the roofs of the
houses of the gods who have learned there are no endings,
only beginnings. That day so hot, heat danced in waves
off bright car tops, we both stood poised at that door
from the east, listened for a long time to the sound of our
grandmothers' voices, the brushing wind of sacred wings,
the rattle of raindrops in dry gourds. I had to participate in
the dreaming of you into memory, cupped your head in the
bowl of my body as ancestors lined up to give you a name
made of their dreams cast once more into this stew of
precious spirit and flesh. And let you go, as I am letting
you go once more in this ceremony of the living, thirteen
years later. And when you were born I held you wet and
unfolding, like a butterfly newly born from the chrysalis
of my body. And breathed with you as you breathed your
first breath. Then was your promise to take it on like the
rest of us, this immense journey, for love, for rain.

BETSY SHOLL

Sex Ed

Well-dressed, demure, jammed into those
politely arranged desks, it's hard to be
serious, but we are. No one even parts lips
to acknowledge what used to drive us crazy
in the back seats of cars, what kept us up
half the night reliving the last slow dance,
girl on her toes, guy bent at the knees
to press in against her.

The instructors speak precisely about
the importance of our children knowing the facts,
so surely none of us in our high heels and
neck ties is going to admit how our first mistakes
have suddenly blossomed so tender and lovely
we've been forgiven a thousand times,
a thousand times forgiven and repeated ourselves.

But fingering the graffiti on this desk,
I remember being braille to you, being read
like a steamy novel, and how those lessons
stayed with us, practical as driver's ed, those hours
of simulation behind the wheel of a parked car.
The truth is I don't regret having studied with you
though I do feel inarticulate, like an athlete
asked to speak in a room of kids, who has nothing
to say except, "practice, practice."

Once our daughter watched the cat in heat
yowl and slither across the floor, and without
looking up asked, would that happen to her. Sometimes
it isn't shame that makes us speechless. It's not
regret that makes me linger at the curb watching
her toss back her yellow hair and yank open
the heavy doors to school.

SHEILA BENDER

With Martha at Gig Harbor

God gives every woman just one sister really
but he mixes them up in families.
We found each other 15 years ago in Madison.
Four years we tucked our dreams between the same
concrete blocks of a dorm room, fear churning
our stomachs, adulthood flattened in front of us
like bags for air turbulence distress.

Today in Gig Harbor you are booking
a Dutch jazz quartet. I've just read
poems across the Narrows in Tacoma.
We are far from 1970 when you left
for Florida believing the South as foreign
as any country and I headed into that state
called early marriage where in the name of love
and heritage we build a park at a dead end.
Slow Children was the only sign posted.

Thirsty for any turn, I asked you for words
and *car, telephone, orchid, water*
became a horoscope I wrote for you.
What is in the stars is this friendship
when few things last a lifetime.
Even the bridge we'll cross tonight heading
to our separate homes replaces one that rippled
once like my children's scarves in wind.
Making waves, making the waves we make,
we are not torn apart.

It is dusk: An elderly man and his wife
negotiate their remote-control model of a yacht
from the steps at water's edge. "Look out,
seaweed ahead," she yells with so much fondness
I picture Jockey shorts in the wicker laundry basket,

lemonade in tall Queen of Hearts glasses.
These people are tickled with the power
to make something come back, something like love,
like our friendship shaking itself dry,
putting the air back in its wings.

ALLISON JOSEPH

Screen Test

They don't make movies
like this anymore, Mother would say
in delight, smiling as another
late-night movie filled
the television screen,
a splashy Esther Williams musical
replete with floating chorus girls
suspended in garish blue water.
Dismissing today's actors
with a wave of her hand,
she'd purse her lips in disgust
over Eddie Murphy's Beverly Hills
antics, Sly Stallone's gun-toting
machismo. *I wouldn't lose*
a moment's sleep to watch
any of them, she'd say, but
would stay up all night
to watch actors whose names
she made sure I knew:
tough guys Raft and Cagney
stalking gangland territory,
proud cowboys Alan Ladd and Randolph Scott
poised for sharpshooting, romantic leads
brooding in tight close-ups—Olivier
and Oberon pacing the desolate moors,
Robert Taylor and Greta Garbo
cinching passion in *Camille*.
And the musicals, with their
flimsy plots and hokey dialogue,
didn't escape her attention either—
Judy and Mickey hoofing it
on endless soundstages,
Rogers and Astaire bickering
everywhere but the dance floor,

or the sexy limbs of Cyd Charisse
flashing stealthily past.

But Mother never mentioned
the luminous beauty of Dorothy
Dandridge, the fine brown frame
of the young Ethel Waters,
or the café-au-lait charm
of matinee idol Lorenzo Tucker,
never commented on Robeson's
stoic strength. Never did she
detail the ugly parody
of blackface, so I was stunned
to find photos of stars from
Judy and Mickey to Shirley Temple
with monstrous, darkened faces.
Mother only seemed to know
the lovely Lena Horne,
who'd appear briefly in white films,
draped in nightclub satin to
sing one number, then disappear.
Only later did I learn
that movie theatres in the South
would snip out Lena's scenes,
her beige beauty offensive
to audiences accustomed
to the catty ways and ploys
of a chain-smoking Bette Davis.

Mother, I am learning now
for us both, captivated
as you surely would have been
had the late-night movie
had some color to it,
other than maids, cooks, fools.
You would have been thrilled
to see splendid Hazel Scott
caressing piano keys,
jazzing the classics with

skilled brown hands,
dynamic Katherine Dunham
dancing fervent on strong legs,
leading her troupe in authentic
African dance, vampy Nina Mae McKinney
seductive and quick as temptation
in an all-singing, all-dancing
all-black musical called *Hallelujah.*
We could have watched together,
seen faces like ours
illuminated on screen
for the whole world to watch.

ANNE RICHEY

Blue Thread

She crushes his pajamas to her face
again, inhaling what can only be musty
after so many years in a box,

then hands them to me like a sacred relic.
Their thinness pains me, their faded, anonymous
look of old clothes in a thrift store bin

people sort through with their minds
elsewhere. She watches me pick at the frayed
facings, the pointless little pocket

that had covered her brother's heart.
She smiles, lets me take my time.
Your sixth-grade graduation dress, remember?

I point to a hem of dogged and delicate stitches.
I used the same blue thread on these.
The same blue as his veins, I almost say,

before they collapsed—how I knew he was gone.
And so I'd eased his sweaty arms and legs
(I remember, she says) from these pajamas

to wash him, clasped the salt-sweet child
to my breast like a newborn
and, counting his fingers and toes,

cried for his perfection (she is stroking
my hand), then laid him on the bed and tried
to think, *I am trying to think*, I say,

how to begin.

LAURA STEARNS

Ice Cabbages

for Ellen

Seventeen when she fled Estonia,
your mother bribed Russian soldiers
with vodka. In Dresden, cathedrals collapsed
like paper parasols in wind.
Steerage to Ellis Island,
a husband from Latvia, the house
that always smelled of blood sausage and tortes.
Forty-five years later she is going back
and you are afraid.

I remember the only family picture you own:
flourdust faces from a country you fear.
Stories rationed through your childhood—
the uncle who drowned himself in the river,
the grandmother who filled a wooden cradle
with corncob dolls after her third stillborn
and a winter of frozen trees.
The gristmill that ground in their sleep.

I see your mother and her sister,
two birds behind the gauze cloth
draped over the wire cage every evening.
I see her suitcase torn open
like a yearly letter, news from namesakes
you will never meet.
Her passport has been pulled from her purse.

In grade school my mother told
her classmates her birth records
were burned in the San Francisco fire,
because her father was from Hungary
and ashamed. We are the daughters

who want to heal our mothers.
I see ice cabbages on the stoop
and want to chip all the way to the heart.
I want the broth I cook to be sorry.
I want our mothers to drink this
until their stomachs are full.

BARBARA LAU

What I Know, What I Haven't Begun to Know

for Mother

If I could hide in the folds of your skirt, just listening;

If I were the cigarettes you lit and lit, that fit between your
fingers
like a sixth digit, a tin sword, an ellipsis to your life;

If I were the crowded steamer that carried you across the
Pacific
to join your military husband, no obstetrician on board and
six months pregnant;

If I were the fake tortoise comb you wore for twenty years
(the same comb, the same French twist);

If I were the bottle you hid beneath the couch, visiting four/
five times a night,
kissing the rim, the warm whiskey tongue, for who knows
how long
you hid it so well;

If I were the hymns you played on church-less Sundays on
your play-by-numbers
organ (*oh rock of ages oh holy holy holy oh Jesus loves me*)
in the corner of the room;

If I were the basket of bougainvillea on your porch that final
summer, heavy
with nursing bees, listening for the snip of your pinking
shears, the jingle
of your instant ice tea;

If I were the moment you knew the doctors were all liars or
    cowards, that it wasn't
epilepsy stroking your body but the sheer, white, evening-
    gloved fingers of death;

If I were the gardenia I would have handed you on my
    wedding day—
(both laughing, both suddenly shy)—me plucking off one
    petal and rubbing it,
first on your neck, then mine.

MILLICENT BORGES

The Last Borges

Like God and his Eve,
you never passed on
your secrets; I struggled
to learn.

Never sure which accent to
migrate towards; which windowpane
to breathe on for the best cursive fog.
I shunned the loud
Portuguese fights.

The visiting relatives, named for saints,
over and over, in the driveway
at night, drunken Uncle John or Paul
or Robert crashed his truck
into the side of our house:

While you went to night school
two nights a week—for twenty years,
and ate linguisa sandwiches,
I watched and listened.

I would catch you: sitting at
Rudy the barber's chair,
I would sneak up behind to hear
foreign words.

At school, I pronounced our name
as you taught me to,
as an Englishman would:
flat and plain, rhyming it with
a word for "pretty."

After a while it seemed
that someone else
had heard a grandmother's
lullabies at night:
a verse that sounded like
a baby's cries for milk,
wanting the nipple:
Ma Ma yo Quedo. Ma Ma yo Quedo.

As you grow older, papa,
I long for a language that joins us,
beyond our last name,
the space between our front teeth,
and wavy black hair.
Beyond linguisa,
kale soup and sweet bread.

But the only Portuguese words
you ever gave me do not stand for love.
Que Careshe. Que Caresh . . .
Son of a bitch. Son of a bitch.

DENISE DUHAMEL

On Being Born the Same Exact Day of the Same Exact Year as Boy George

We must have clamored for the same mother, hurried for the same womb.
I know it now as I read that my birthday is his.
Since the first time I saw his picture, I sensed something—
and with a fierce bonding and animosity
began following his career.

Look where I am and look where he is!
There is a book documenting his every haircut
while all my image-building attempts go unnoticed, even by my friends.
I'm too wimpy to just dye my curls red
or get them straightened. I, sickening and moral,

talked about chemicals when I should have been
hanging out with George's pal, Marilyn.
He would have set me right:
Stop your whining and put on this feather tuxedo. Look,
do you want to be famous or not?

In the latest articles, Boy George is claiming he's not
really happy. Hmm, I think, just like me.
When he comes to New York and stays at hotels in Gramercy Park
maybe he feels a pull to the Lower East Side,
wanders towards places where I am, but not knowing me, doesn't know why.

One interviewer asks if he wishes he were a woman.
Aha! I read on with passion: and a poet? Boy, I bet you'd like that—

You wouldn't have to sing anymore, do those tiring tours.
George, we could switch. You could come live at my place,
have some privacy, regain your sense of self.

So I begin my letter. Dear Boy George,
Do you ever sit and wonder what's gone wrong?
If there's been some initial mistake?
Well, don't be alarmed. There has been,
but I can set it straight.

PATRICIA VALDATA

New Jersey Turnpike: Exit 14

At dusk, from the hotel room,
I can just make out the lights
Of the Outerbridge Crossing. The Verrazano
Fades into the dirty cape of brown haze that hangs
Over the shoulders of the city. Rush-hour traffic
Fills northbound and southbound roads,
Spills onto entrance ramps,
Clogs deceleration lanes.
Aloft, the landing lights of inbound jets
Look like planets strung along the ecliptic.
The airliners land, turn off their lights,
Taxi past the old grey terminal.

Child of the fifties, I was proud of
That terminal building: The Newarker
Restaurant, the electric billboard's rotating panels,
Machines that dispensed cheap flight insurance.
It was the stuff of grade school reports
Printed in block letters on construction
Paper, blue for sky, grey for planes,
Bound with brass fasteners behind a yellow cover,
Full of facts culled from dated encyclopedias:
Transportation, Modern. Read
From east to west: the port's enormous cranes,
Chains of boxcars strung atop railroad tracks,
A highway not yet expanded to twelve lanes,
The long runway.
I like riding through this confluence of cargo,
Disgusted by the stench of refineries
But knowing it all to be signs of Progress, Modern.

Nostalgia spills as I stare at the cars
Creeping up the turnpike; this is, after all,
Home. Suddenly I long for an egg bagel

With lox and cream cheese, hard Italian rolls,
Subs made without pickles, without mayonnaise,
The edible artifacts of my childhood. But
I don't really want to stay here; there's
Too much pavement, too many people.

In the fading light, the Empire State Building
Stands up like a Redstone rocket, reminding me
Of trips to the airport, all of us in the Chevy,
My father driving, my mother smoking her Salems,
My aunt and cousin squeezed in the backseat with me.
We're dropping him at the airport, he's going
All the way to Illinois to college.
As the roadbed rises into viaduct over
The streets of Elizabeth, I have to spot
The clock on the facade of the funeral home
Or it's bad luck.
The plane could crash.
It would be my fault.
As my father slows for the exit,
I stare out the window at the runway,
Watching the turboprop accelerate,
Imagining the takeoff.

MAUREEN SEATON

Mortal Sins

Aldo Palmieri straddles
the back seat of the schoolbus,
chainsmokes Luckys like a cowboy.
I'm fifteen.
I love his pathos, his acne,
his yellow-stained fingers.
JFK dies during study hall.
Jane Murphy gets pregnant, leaves
school. I take phenobarbital daily
for my nerves.

At sixteen my face falls into place
around my nose.
I meet Harvey Brotman underwater
at the Jones Beach pool.
We share whoppers with cheese in Franklin Square.
His parents say: "One date with a Catholic
girl is too much."
I think Harvey is making this up.

I'm seventeen:
long hair, brace-less teeth.
I worship Kevin Duffy, boast
his fraternity pin
on my Peter Pan collar.
I think kissing is a mortal sin.
I think holding hands is possibly
a mortal sin.
Father Reilly says: "Watch out! Holding hands
is a venial that could easily lead
to a mortal."
Kevin drops me for a "Popover Girl" from Patricia Murphy's
who giggles whenever a car with one headlight
passes by.

I meet my husband-to-be at the Ship Ahoy
in New Rochelle, acquire a taste for scotch;
at eighteen, trade eternity
for a good french kiss.
I learn to cook Thanksgiving dinner
for twenty in-laws, put on weight,
take it off, put it on, learn
my husband prefers blondes.

I'm thirty-one:
the year of designer jeans.
My ass is finally "in."
I get my ears double-pierced,
cut six inches off my hair, let it grow
on my legs, under my arms.
I take my daughter to the Twin Towers.
We look down, say, "Wow."
She holds my face in her baby hands,
says: "You're so pretty, Mommy."
I laugh.
She tells me again & again
until one day, I am.

HARRIET JACOBS

growing into my name

for harriet tubman

worn like a hand-me-down
unfashionable   unasked for
a quiet stitching of syllables
apart   from the boisterous crowd
of cheryls jackies and debbies
you oldwoman ghost ridin hard
on my young girl shoulders
wasn't no soft name i was given / no
something about the cadence
or maybe it was the weight of history marching across the
    tongue
that held me captive
disallowing total escape
into the mindlessness of youth
until somewhere in me
i remembered
now i pray
and stretch my heart and limbs
to fit this cloak painted with the nameless faces
of stars
the sound of your name steady as my own breath
your iron will knitting my spine
i hear the rush of secrets
in your eyes and
now
i cannot look at the sky
without seeing your name spelled out
in the passing of clouds
over the moon
danger has a familiar smell about it
and on moonless nights

i put candles in my hair
and wait
by the side of the road

LAUREL MILLS

Learning Our Names

The sun anchors us to this spot, knows
our first touch. Shielded by sumac,
the tiny meadow hums with longing.
A yellow jacket buzzes between us—
piece of striped sunlight.

When you reach toward me, the day,
like a thin jar, cracks. All our lives
we've readied for this moment.

The marriages we endured:
Seven-up spiked with bourbon to muzzle
hunger whining in my heart like a hurt dog,
long sleeves to hide welts on your arms.

Illumined here are Queen Anne's lace
and the slow spiral of a spider
on transparent thread.

With a tremulous finger, you trace
my ankle, the line of my arch.
I stroke the underside of your arm:
flesh soft, sweet as pollen
in the throat of a lily.

JUDITH VOLLMER

from Wildsisters Bar

After Friedan & the flare
of Millett, the rebirth
of the presses & clinics,
after the Seneca Encampment,
after Kirkpatrick & Thatcher,
after welfare women remain unrescued,
I go to bed wondering why
we'll try to build a *women's space*
in the middle of a depression,
the grand notions of our art
boiling & simmering on a stove
with one working burner.

How do you operate a jackhammer if
you've never owned a toolbox?
Who knows how to vent a stinking drain?
Those questions and the pleasing ones—
can we invite the Roches
to do a gig soon?—
pound at us while we build fire walls, sand chairs, replace wiring.
The unemployed guitarist who lives upstairs
solemnly agrees that Neil Young is the father of punk.
We move on to Grace Jones,
Grace Slick. May the mother of punk
be with us forever,
her fierce and beautiful curls
forever in our faces.
Neighborhood men drop by the hundred-year-old
building while we work, give us the raised fist.
How's the *sisterhood* going? Slowly. According
to Rita, who hasn't seen a paycheck in 90 days
and works this project between bus trips
to the welfare line, the work is moving.

DENISE DUHAMEL

Feminism

All over the world, Little Bees, Star Scouts,
and Blue Birds play Telephone, whispering messages
in a chain link of ears—no repeating (that's cheating),
only relaying what they hear their first shot.
Sometimes "Molly loves Billy" becomes "A Holiday in Fiji,"
or "Do the Right Thing" becomes "The Man Who Would Be
King."
Still, there is trust. Girls taking the Blind Walk,
a bandana around one's eyes (Pin the Tail on the Donkey–
style)
as another leads her through the woods
or a back yard or entire city blocks. Girls helping
where they are needed or inventing ways to aid
where they seemingly are not. Memorizing remedies
for cuts and stings, frostbite, nosebleeds.
Their motto: Be prepared at all times.
Full of anxiety, they watch for home hazards,
check for frayed toaster or hair dryer cords.
Outside they watch for color changes in cloud formations,
the darkening of the sky. They're safest in cars
during electrical storms.
There's so much to remember and
learn.
So many impending disasters, yet so many well wishes
for their world. These girls shut the tap
as they brush their teeth, secure glow-in-the-dark reflectors
on their bikes, and do at least one good turn daily.
They are taught that alone they are small,
but if they can empathize with each other, they can gain
power.
Just to see what it feels like, a walking girl
may spend an afternoon in a wheelchair. Another
may stuff cotton in her ears. And to be readied
for what lies ahead when they grow up

and they're no longer Girl Scouts, they make collages
cutting images from magazines showing what they might be:
mothers or lawyers, reporters or nurses.
Or they play Rabbit Without A House, a Brazilian form
of London Bridge, or American Musical Chairs.
There will always be an odd number of girls, always
one left out. The earth and her scarce resources.
Survival in Sudan begins with Sheep And Hyena.
And though the girls may try to protect the one
who is the Sheep in the middle of their circle, most often
the outside Hyena does not give up
and breaks through sore forearms and weakened wrists
to eat her. Red Rover, Red Rover,
it is better when Girl Scouts stay together.
So they bond tightly in their Human Knot,
a female version of the football team's huddle.
And all holding hands, they squeeze their Friendship
    Squeeze,
knowing each small one-at-a-time grip
is like a Christmas tree light, each a twinkle
the rest of the strand cannot do without.
Each missing face on the missing child poster
like the fairest of all looking into her mirror.

MARY WEEMS

Return to Temptation

After hearing about the death of Melvin Franklin, of the Temptations

Melvin's dead,
a cloud-nine moves
a 4-step sway to the left
in 5-part harmony,
the sun shines at half-mast,
silent nights have a fit.

Melvin's dead.
I am 13 again
sitting in new beginner
bra, first stockings
and heels, facing
the stage at Leo's Casino
holding my breath.
The space darkens and David,
doo glistening like black
magic, sequined lapel flashing
moonlight, steps up letting a smooth
note float from a mouth
made for singing.
"Sonny," and Temptation
fills the room
like new money.
I watch, throat dry
as fall leaves, as Eddie,
Melvin, Otis, and Paul
fall into steps so together
they are one movement.

Melvin's dead.
The psychedelic shack opens,

filled with spirits
chanting
"psychedelic shack that's where it's at
psychedelic shack that's where it's at"
champagne popping corks
like banana-brown fingers,
punch spiked
with shaking boodies
and doo-wops bubbling.

Melvin's dead.
I want to ride
on Ol' Man River
carve out a canoe
bare fingers bleeding
yesterday.
Paddle into his heart
pump it up
pump it up
pump it up
so full of love
it rises.
Grab one of them 9 lives
God gives cats
on a regular basis
so Melvin can get
back in line
back in step
let out a single
note—
return to
Temptation.

KATHY MANGAN

St. Paul Street Seasonal

Not the crocuses, sporadic
purple and yellow stars in row house
yards, not the ice-cream wrappers
stuck to the sidewalks,

but the syringe—
someone's discarded joy—
nestled in the green
new shoots of our ivy

trumpets the Baltimore spring.
Dusks, the halfway house
spills its wounded, who shuffle
and spout soliloquies

while their keepers shepherd them
towards the deli for sugared coffee
and crullers. The sex-chatter
of the university students, sprung

at midnight from the library
and formulas and anatomy, wafts
through our second-story screen,
spicing our sleep. In the slant

of 10 A.M. sun, the scarecrow man—
all folded slats and angles—now daily
stations his wheelchair outside
the newsstand and opens his hand

like a time-lapse tulip
for my quarter, the palm
of his fingerless glove so grimy
it shines.

PAULA SERGI

Sound Flying into and out of My Ears

I don't know if it's white, like the one
that lived in the tall blue spruce in back
of our childhood home, this bird whose voice
flies into and out of my ears all night.
We were afraid of that owl, imagined
he could see all the way behind his head.
My sister cut ads for cigars, pictures from bird books,
hid them to startle me; when I reached
for simple items, socks and tee shirts,
looked under my pillow, in drawers and closets,
the image of a white owl appeared.

But the one who sings to me now
owns the hollow of my heart, the place
empty still, despite lovers and sisters,
husband and children. He listens for
the echo there, a constant "who?"
Longs to hear his voice resonate
in a chamber, hovers for a place to nest.

This morning, after three nights
of waking to the chant, a long, loud call
always followed by a soft one,
I walked to the river looking for him,
searched potential nesting places, dark mesh
in bare trees against the light grey sky,
large notes hanging on a barren scale.
I hoped to see his silhouette, big as a cat,
perched on the dead limbs of a sycamore.

Today, nothing stirs, so nothing rests.
It's as silent as a snow-filled river path,
silent as an owl's flight. By noon the quiet

will have covered my footprints, erasing
my search. Tonight, owl sounds will thread
through my ears like ribbons in a weave
of wanting.

ELIZABETH ALEXANDER

Affirmative Action Blues (1993)

Right now two black people sit in a jury room
in Southern California trying to persuade
nine white people that what they saw when four white
police officers brought batons back like
they were smashing a beautiful piñata was
"a violation of Rodney King's civil rights,"
just as I am trying to convince my boss not ever
to use the word "niggardly" in my presence again.
He's a bit embarrassed, then asks, but don't you know
the word's etymology? as if that makes it
somehow not the word, as if a word can't batter.
Never again for as long as you live, I tell him,
and righteously. Then I dream of a meeting
with my colleagues where I scream so loud the inside
of my skull bleeds, and my face erupts in scabs.
In the dream I use an office which is overrun
with mice, rats, and round-headed baby otters
who peer at me from exposed water pipes (and somehow
I know these otters are Negroes), and my boss says,
Be grateful, your office is bigger than anyone
else's, and maybe if you kept it clean you wouldn't
have those rats. And meanwhile, black people are dying,
beautiful black men my age, from AIDS. It was amazing
when I learned the root of "venereal disease"
was "Venus," that there was such a thing as a disease
of love. And meanwhile, poor Rodney King can't think
    straight;
what was knocked into his head was some addled notion
of love his own people make fun of, "Can we all
get along? Please?" You can't hit a lick with a crooked
stick; a straight stick made Rodney King believe he was
not a piñata, that amor vincit omnia.
I know I have been changed by love.
I know that love is not a political agenda, it lacks sustained

analysis, and we can't dance our way out of our constrictions.

I know that the word "niggardly" is "of obscure etymology" but probably derived from the French Norman, and that Chaucer and Milton and Shakespeare used it. It means "stingy," and the root is not the same as "nigger," which derives from "negar," meaning black, but they are perhaps, perhaps, etymologically related. The two "g"s are two teeth gnawing; rodent is from the Latin "rodere," which means "to gnaw," as I have said elsewhere.

I know so many things, including the people who love me and the people who do not.

In Tourette's syndrome you say the very thing that you are thinking, and then a word is real.

These are words I have heard in the last 24 hours which fascinate me: "vermin," "screed," "carmine," and "niggardly."

I am not a piñata, Rodney King insists. Now can't we all get along?

JOYCE SUTPHEN

Crossroads

The second half of my life will be black
to the white rind of the old and fading moon.
The second half of my life will be water
over the cracked floor of these desert years.
I will land on my feet this time,
knowing at least two languages and who
my friends are. I will dress for the
occasion, and my hair shall be
whatever color I please.
Everyone will go on celebrating the old
birthday, counting the years as usual,
but I will count myself new from this
inception, this imprint of my own desire.

The second half of my life will be swift,
past leaning fenceposts, a gravel shoulder,
asphalt tickets, the beckon of open road.
The second half of my life will be wide-eyed,
fingers sifting through fine sands,
arms loose at my sides, wandering feet.
There will be new dreams every night,
and the drapes will never be closed.
I will toss my string of keys into a deep
well and old letters into the grate.

The second half of my life will be ice
breaking up on the river, rain
soaking the fields, a hand
held out, a fire,
and smoke going
upward, always up.

CAROL DORF

Sara's Daughters

We're Sara's daughters, middle-aged
women at the Fertility Clinic,
waiting, while a husband's middle-aged
sperm is washed of semen and sugared
to sweeten its path to the egg.

Sometimes they let us wait outside the lab
so we don't surreptitiously watch
the full ones lumber in and out, stopping
in sudden attention to a particularly
strong series of kicks and elbowings.

This is a monthly story, that begins with playing
scientist in your own bathroom, ends
with crying at the sight of blood, as though
we were unfamiliar with blood. Each month,
we long for an angel to hover over our beds.

JEANNE BRYNER

Butterfly

The thing I keep thinking is these young men
are much too weak to make love.
These boys with yellow hair and blue tattoos
and bristly mustaches who are married
and dying with AIDS cannot enter each other
in the old way—bony hips hang,
unbeautiful, too tired to pump.

Like soft cowbells their hoop earrings
tinkle in ER, room thirteen,
as they press cool cloths to foreheads,
pass tissues for sticky green phlegm.
They wait for the doctor and lab techs
and nurses who mark their plastic name bands
with a *B*. *B* for *blood hazard*, *B* for *boys*,
B for *bad*. Orange-ball stickers tag
their charts; flags go up that say DANGER.

I am their nurse, and when they ask
for blankets, they cover each other the way
I spread quilts on my daughter in her crib.

They are half a butterfly on grey cement;
their skin shrinks and tarnishes,
bodies cave in, revival tents
collapsing the final week of summer.

They cough as I enter their room,
and something in me stiffens.
Even this far away in my mask and gown
and gloves trying hard to say—*I care*
that you suffer, that your cottage burns—
its flames reach inside my tent. Whatever
chokes in this fire is large and soundless and pale.

I keep thinking as these men lift each other's
heads from the pillow, gently tilt straws
close to dusky lips, hold hands as needles
dig for veins and pull and straighten
hospital sheets hour after wounded hour—
they are migrating back to the cocoon,
the place where brown masks
protect the unbeautiful.

JUDITH HOUGEN

Fitness Club: Riding the Lifecycle

We're as fat as we are dishonest.–Judi Hollis

The control panel counts time, calories, miles
gone, outlining hills to come, the red lights
beating calmly, saying, *the place you need to go*
is at least 15 pounds from here, how willing

are you? mile after mile. I could have pedaled
these phantom wheels across America by now.
Anchored to this amputee of the modern age,
I give away the last thickness of fat to computerized

inclines, to a blinding honesty that must negotiate
with everything I see. After years of struggling through
a life fed by half-truths, I am laying down the past like
the careful molasses of asphalt: a thick, methodical

roadway. It doesn't solve everything, but it's real.
I am willing to hold the sad weight of every lie
I told while raging at the world through my body.
These days, movement is no longer

optional. I have learned to welcome
the sanity of each mile, to love the woman
inside this engine who reinvents the wheel
daily and now has important places to go.

CYNTHIA GALLAHER

Trying on Marilyn Monroe's Shoes

I said, "Girl, like when did Marilyn ever walk *around* in
these?
C'mon, she just stood under flood lights
and looked beautiful, let noisy black cameras wink at her,
then found herself whisked away to her next
appointment by limo."

"Or hearse," said the Latvian actress
from Kalamazoo, here in this Chicago loft gallery,
and the current owner of the Marilyn Monroe vintage shoes.
"I went to school with a lot of Latvians," I offered.
"That's strange," said a Puerto Rican artist,
"I went to school with a lot of *Latin Kings*."

The actress continued, ignoring him, "These shoes
were hardly worn at all.
Lilac, baby doll, four-inch chunk heel.
They just scream Marilyn and the 50s, don't they?"
And I mused, "Shouldn't every girl have at least
one pair of special shoes in her lifetime?"
Even toothpick-leg girls like me—
why my mother would spy me through the kitchen window
walking home from school and say,
"Honey, what are those two strings
hanging from the bottom of your dress?"

But even thread-leg girls go to the prom,
and we girls bought the cheapest
white cloth shoes from Malings
dyed to match a swatch cut from our prom dress seams.
The tinting happened in the back room
of the shoe store, a clerk straddling a footstool
holding a dripping dauber under fluorescent lights,
with shoes never matching exactly when he was done.

But Marilyn's shoes were of the smoothest leather,
with perfect, nearly invisible seams, and a one-of-a-kind
  lilac,
made just for Marilyn.

"If they *were* a standard size," I asked, " which would they
  be?"
"I don't know, seven or seven-and-a-half,"
said the Latvian, on tour in a
multilingual production and good at translation.
The number danced like winning lotto in my head.
"Let me try them on," I said, and
slipped off black Chinese slippers,
and in stretch pants,
almost like the pedal pushers of the 50s,
raising one stick leg at a time,
though now subjected to more than a year
of stair climbing, cycling, treadmill
and weight machines,
I stepped into Marilyn's shoes,
did three pirouettes in the empty gallery;

and friend Ginny gasped,
"Why girl, you've got a pair of legs on you!
Have *you* got the legs!"
And just as suddenly, the shoes gave me curvy calves,
expressive thighs, even a behind.

And Sandra, didn't that happen to Esperanza
and her friends on Mango Street
when they were twelve, dirty legged and snot nosed,
trying on those candy-colored shoes they found in the alley,
suddenly drawing whistles
from newspaper boys and bums?
And me, always a late bloomer,
now at the same age Marilyn died,
I finally have legs.

To Leslie—
Keep walking in words—
It's fun.
Cynthia Gallaher

Stay with me,
my overnight successes, both,
click your heels together,
cut, print it, save the reel,
even after I slip those shoes off.

BARBARA CROOKER

Nearing Menopause, I Run into Elvis at Shoprite

near the peanut butter. He calls me ma'am, like the sweet
southern mother's boy he was. This is the young Elvis,
slim-hipped, dressed in leather, black hair swirled
like a duck's backside. I'm in the middle of my life,
the start of the body's cruel betrayals, the skin beginning
to break in lines and creases, the thickening midline.
I feel my temperature rising, as a hot flash washes over,
the thermostat broken down. The first time I heard Elvis
on the radio, I was poised between girlhood and what comes
next.
My parents were appalled, in the Eisenhower fifties, by rock
and roll and all it stood for, let me only buy one record,
"Love Me Tender," and I did.
I have on a tight orlon sweater, circle skirt,
eight layers of rolled-up net petticoats, all bound
together by a woven straw cinch belt. Now I've come
full circle, hate the music my daughter loves, Nine
Inch Nails, Smashing Pumpkins, Crash Test Dummies.
Elvis looks embarrassed for me. His soft full lips
are like moon pies, his eyelids half-mast, pulled
down bedroom shades. He mumbles, "Treat me nice."
Now, poised between menopause and what comes next, the
last
dance, I find myself in tears by the toilet paper rolls,
hearing "Unchained Melody" on the sound system. "That's
all
right now, Mama," Elvis says, "Anyway you do is fine." The
bass
line thumps and grinds, the honky-tonk piano moves like
an ivory
river, full of swampy delta blues. And Elvis's voice wails above
it all, the purr and growl, the snarl and twang, above the
chains
of flesh and time.

Self-Portrait at Eighty with Twelve-String

Out of the corner of her good eye she recognizes it
  tonight on television: there it is, she's sure of it,

her old Martin dazzling as a dozen wild yellow lilies
  opening on stage in a younger woman's arms—this guitar

home once to a spider crawling out of the center
  hole, the fiberglass case unlatched after a long winter

to reveal the plush lining, this guitar that slept under
  shooting stars, that arose over white water—a woman
  young

enough (she thinks though she never had children)
  to be her great-granddaughter with peacock feather

earrings and Joplinesque hair, who puts 5,000 miles
  on her car in a week driving from Boston

up to Prince Edward Island and back in search of America—
  this guitar of bald tires and all-nighters with fast

friends at the wheel, of ferryboat queues and camping out
  on fragrant deserted beaches—a woman still

a girl recklessly singing in Canada at sunrise, her sleeping
  bag wet from the flood tide, feeling again the raw

action of silk and steel cutting octave lines
  into her fingertips, and the heat of a handrolled

joint being passed, the orange ashes falling too fast
    on the angelic rosewood face whose black scar

the size of a seed pearl just inches below the neck
    suddenly burns in the blue light of the screen.

Let Go

Unfasten your belt. Let your stomach out.
Let it lower. Let it grow. Unbraid the braid.
Shake your hair out. Blow your nose. Spit.
The pantyhose—off, pantygirdle—off, panties—off.
Cut the straps of your bra with a jackknife.
Say *blah* and *blech* and break plates.
Break them into the basement.
Throw out the old food. Precious jellies and jams,
precious watermelon pickle—flush them.
Razor blade the snake bite and let the poison out.
Say *dah* and *duh* and *don't.*
Pour the crap out of the vacuum cleaner bag.
Scatter the manure over the weeds and pull up
the rose bushes by the roots.
Burst the seedpods of milkweeds, unhinge
the snapdragons from their stems. Clip
the hedges down to the bone and burn
the new growth and the old growth together
on a bonfire. Throw your animal skin underwear
in there, too, the ones you wore in high school
before you had a soul. The elbow-high gloves,
the pumps dyed apricot to match the trim of the dress,
the crown, the dried corsage. Bible-pressed and sad,
burn them, burn them and yelp. Say *yah.* Say *uh.*
The old and new tampons, the old blue boxes of Kotex,
the hieroglyphic mattress pads, the family photographs
and the baby hair flattened in envelopes, butterfly
collections,
the precious wings of the luna moth, and the pins, all the
pins,
straight and safety and bobby and hat, the patterns,
the corduroy and velvet and unused bridesmaids' dresses,
the newspapers claiming victory and the newspapers
claiming defeat,

the headless Venus and the armless Buddha and the Pietà
made of plaster and beads, the death masks of Egyptians
and the fingerbones of saints, the surgical staples and scars,
the umbilical cords saved in jars, fetal chickens and cow
    hearts
from old science projects, diaphragms, rubbers, old moans
and new groans, glances, romances, beauty and guilt, regret,
remorse, rebates and rejuvenations, east, west, south and
    north,
break through the cobwebs with a broom, cut through
the weaving-in-progress on the hand-made loom,
unfeather the loon and the voice of the loon, dismember
the stories, the sternness of fact, the howlings of dogs,
the screamings of cats, let the trains clack till they fall
in the sea, dismember the dandelion, unhoney the bee,
release the old thunder, the old unspoken storms,
spit the seeds high of the apple and pear, uncover
the caskets, throw the bones in the air
throw the bones in the air
throw the bones in the air
and cut off your hair.

Contributors' Notes

LIZ ABRAMS-MORLEY was born in 1951. Her poems have appeared in several journals and anthologies, and her chapbook, *Memory Waltz*, was published in 1995. A trained family therapist, she is also a frequent poet-in-residence in area schools near her home in Pennsylvania.

KIM ADDONIZIO was born in Washington, D.C., in 1954. Her first poetry collection, *The Philosopher's Club*, received the 1994 Great Lakes New Writers Award and a silver medal from the Commonwealth Club of California; she has also received two fellowships from the National Endowment for the Arts. Her latest collection is *Jimmy & Rita* (1997), and she is coauthor, with Dorianne Laux, of *The Poet's Companion: A Guide to the Pleasures of Writing Poetry*.

ELIZABETH ALEXANDER is the author of three books of poetry, *The Venus Hottentot*, *Body of Life*, and the forthcoming *Neonatology*. She is currently the Grace Hazard Conkling Poet-in-Residence and director of the Poetry Center at Smith College.

JULIA ALVAREZ is a poet, essayist, and fiction writer who spent her early childhood in the Dominican Republic. In 1991 she published *How the Garcia Girls Lost Their Accents*, which won a PEN Oakland Award and was selected as a notable book by the *New York Times* and the *American Library Journal*. Her second novel, *In the Time of the Butterflies*, was a finalist for the National Book Critics Award in fiction in 1995. She has also published two books of poems: *The Other Side / El Otro Lado* and *Homecoming: New and Collected Poems*. A third novel, *YO!*, was published in January 1997. A collection of essays, *Something to Declare*, was published in 1998. She has just sold her first children's book, *The Secret Footprints*. She lives in Vermont, where she is currently working on a new novel.

DOROTHY BARRESI is the author of *All of the Above*, which won the Barnard New Women Poet's Prize, and *The Post-Rapture Diner*, winner of an American Book Award. Her poems and essays have appeared in a wide variety of literary magazines, and she has received a Pushcart Prize and a National Endowment for the Arts fellowship. She is a professor of English and creative writing at California State University, Northridge, and she lives in the Los Angeles area with her husband and sons.

JACKIE BARTLEY was born in Pittsburgh in 1951. Her second poetry chapbook, *The Terrible Boundaries of the Body*, won the White Eagle Coffee Store Press chapbook contest award in 1996. Her poems have appeared in *Controlled Burn*, *Tar River Poetry*, *West Branch*, and other journals. She lives in Holland, Michigan.

JAN BEATTY is the author of *Mad River*, which won the 1994 Agnes Lynch Starrett Poetry Prize in 1994. She has won the Pablo Neruda Prize for poetry and two fellowships from the Pennsylvania Council on the Arts, and her chapbook, *Ravenous*, won the State Street Press chapbook prize in 1995. In addition to her career as a writer, she has held a variety of jobs, from welfare caseworker to waitress.

JUDY BELSKY was born in Seattle in 1947. She has published a memoir, *Thread of Blue*, and several books for children. Her first poetry manuscript, *Pathworn*, recently won the Rachel Castelete Prize for poetry. She is a clinical psychologist living in Jerusalem.

SHEILA BENDER's newest book of poems is *Sustenance: New and Selected Poems*, and she is also the author of four books on creative writing, including *Writing in a New Convertible with the Top Down*, and *The Writer's Journal: 40 Writers and Their Journals*. She teaches creative writing in the Northwest.

JILL BIALOSKY was born in Cleveland. She received her M.F.A. from the University of Iowa Writers' Workshop and has published poems in the *New Yorker*, *TriQuarterly*, *Seneca Review*, and many other magazines. She has received the Writer's Voice New Poets Award and the Elliot Coleman Award in poetry, and was a finalist for a General Electric Writer's Award. Her first book of poems, *The End of Desire*, was published in 1997, and she has also coedited an anthology, *Wanting a Child*. She is currently an editor at W. W. Norton and lives in New York City with her husband and son.

MILLICENT BORGES was born in Long Beach, California, in 1962. She received a grant from the National Endowment for the Arts (1997–98), and her recent work has appeared in *Tampa Review*, *Seattle Review*, *Laurel Review*, and *Midland Review*. She lives in Venice, California.

MARIANNE BORUCH was born in Chicago in 1950. She is the author of four collections of poetry, *A Stick That Breaks and Breaks*, *Moss Burning*, *Descendant*, and *A View from the Gazebo*. Her book of essays, *Poetry's Old Air*, was published in 1995. She teaches in the M.F.A. program at Purdue University.

JEANNE BRYNER was born in

Waynesburg, Pennsylvania, in 1951. Her chapbook, *Breathless*, was published in 1995. Her work has appeared in a variety of publications, including *Prairie Schooner* and the *Sun*, and has been anthologized in *Between the Heartbeats: Poetry and Prose by Nurses*. The recipient of a 1997 Individual Artist Fellowship from the Ohio Arts Council, she works as an emergency room nurse.

CATHLEEN CALBERT was born in Jackson, Michigan, in 1955. Her first book of poems, *Lessons in Space*, was published in 1997. A second collection, *Bad Judgment*, is forthcoming in 1999. She is an associate professor at Rhode Island College.

MARILYN CHIN was born in Hong Kong in 1955 and raised in Portland, Oregon. She is the author of *Dwarf Bamboo* and *The Phoenix Gone, The Terrace Empty*. She was interviewed in Bill Moyers's *Language of Life*, in which her poetry was also featured. She teaches in the writing program at San Diego State University.

SANDRA CISNEROS was born in Chicago in 1954. Her books of poetry include *My Wicked Wicked Ways*, and *Loose Woman*, winner of a Mountains & Plains Booksellers Association's Regional Book Award. Cisneros is also the author of *The House on Mango Street*, which has sold more than a million copies and is used as a text in classrooms across the country, and *Woman Hollering Creek and Other Stories*, which won the PEN Center West Award for Best Fiction, the Quality Paperback Book Club New Voices Award, and the Lannan Foundation Literary Award, and was also selected a noteworthy book of the year by the *New York Times* and the *American Library Journal*. Her numerous awards include two National Endowment for the Arts fellowships, a Before Columbus American Book Award, and a Chicano Short Story Award from the University of Arizona. She has also been invited twice to read at the Library of Congress, by Poet Laureate Gwendolyn Brooks in 1986 and Poet Laureate Rita Dove in 1995. She lives in San Antonio.

GERALDINE CONNOLLY was born in 1947 in Greensburg, Pennsylvania, and drove a 1964 gold Plymouth Valiant convertible when she was a teenager. She is the author of a chapbook, *The Red Room*, and two full-length poetry collections, *Food for the Winter* and *Province of Fire*. She has won two National Endowment for the Arts fellowships, as well as the Carolyn Kizer Prize from *Poetry Northwest*. She teaches in the Johns Hopkins graduate writing program in Washington, D.C., and serves as executive director of *Poet Lore.*

BARBARA CROOKER was born in Cold Spring, New York, in 1945. Her latest book of poems is *In the Late Summer Garden* (1998). She has received three poetry fellowships from the Pennsylvania Council of the Arts.

SILVIA CURBELO's first collection of poems, *The Secret History of Water*, was published in 1997. She has received poetry fellowships from the National Endowment for the Arts, the Florida Arts Council, and the Cintas Foundation, and was recently awarded the Jessica Nobel-Maxwell Memorial Poetry Prize from *American Poetry Review.* A native of Cuba, she makes her home in Tampa.

KATHRYN DANIELS was born in 1955 and grew up in Natick, Massachusetts. Her poetry and fiction have appeared in numerous literary magazines and in the anthologies *Fine China* and *If I Had a Hammer*, and her fiction has recently been performed as a theatrical monologue. She lives in New York City.

CAROL DORF was born in 1957. Her poetry has been published in a number of magazines, including *13th Moon, Feminist Studies, Mediphors*, and *Five Fingers Review.*

RITA DOVE has had a distinguished career in American literature. Currently on the English department faculty at University of Virginia, she served as Poet Laureate and Consultant in Poetry for the Library of Congress from 1993 to 1995. She is the author of numerous books of poetry, including the recent *On the Bus with Rosa Parks, Mother Love*, and *Thomas and Beulah*; in addition she has also authored essays, plays, short stories, musical collaborations, and a novel. Her many honors include serving as a member of the Afro-American Studies Visiting Committee at Harvard, the Council of Scholars of the Library of Congress, and the Thomas Jefferson Center for the Freedom of Expression. She has also received the Charles Frankel Prize and the National Medal in the Arts from the White House and the National Endowment for the Humanities. She won the Pulitzer Prize for poetry in 1987.

DENISE DUHAMEL was born in Providence, Rhode Island, in 1961. Her most recent book is *The Star-Spangled Banner*, which won the Crab Orchard Review's Poetry Prize. She is also the author of *Exquisite Politics* (a collaborative work with Maureen Seaton), *Kinky, Girl Soldier*, and *How the Sky Fell.* Her work has been widely anthologized, including in three editions of *The Best American Poetry* (1993, 1994, and 1998).

KATHRYN DUNN was born in 1951

and grew up in Gardner, Massachusetts. Her work has appeared in several journals, including *Yankee*. She teaches creative writing in both private and public institutions.

LONNIE HULL DUPONT was born in 1953 in Michigan. She is the author of five chapbooks, and her poems have appeared in such magazines as *Americas Review* and *Rain City Review*. She lives in Ann Arbor, Michigan, where she works as a freelance book editor and writes biographies for young readers.

LYNN EMANUEL is the author of two books of poetry, *Hotel Fiesta* and *The Dig*. She has been the recipient of two National Endowment for the Arts fellowships, the National Poetry Series Award, and three Pushcart prizes, and her poetry has been anthologized in *Best American Poetry*. She was also a poetry editor for the literature panel of the National Endowment for the Arts. She studied with Adrienne Rich at the City College of New York and received an M.F.A. from the University of Iowa. She serves as the director of the writing program at the University of Pittsburgh.

HEID ERDRICH was born right after the death of John F. Kennedy on November 26, 1963. She was the sixth of seven children and grew up in North Dakota, where her parents taught at the Bureau of Indian Affairs boarding school. She is a member of the Turtle Mountain Band of Ojibway. She graduated from Dartmouth College and earned a master's degree from the Johns Hopkins University Writing Seminars. Her first book of poems, *Fishing for Myth*, won a Minnesota Voices Project Award and was nominated for a Minnesota Book Award. She teaches writing and Native American literature at the University of St. Thomas in St. Paul, Minnesota.

KELLY NORMAN ELLIS was born in Illinois in 1964 and raised in "the strong southern world of Jackson, Mississippi." She is a founding member of Affrilachian Poets, a writing ensemble with roots in the Black South of Appalachia, and an assistant professor of creative writing at Chicago State University. Her work has also been anthologized in *Spirit and Flame: Contemporary African American Poetry* (1997).

SUSAN FIRER's third book, *The Lives of the Saints and Everything* (1993), won the Cleveland State University Poetry Center Prize and the Posner Award, and she is also the author of *The Underground Communion Rail* (1992). Her poems have appeared in *Best American Poetry*, *Iowa Review*, *Prairie Schooner*, *Ms.*, and many other journals. She lives in Wisconsin.

CYNTHIA GALLAHER was born in

1953. She is the author of *Swimmer's Prayer*; *Private, On Purpose*; and *Night Ribbons*, which was honored by the Illinois Library Association and the Chicago Public Library.

PAMELA GEMIN was born in Ann Arbor, Michigan, in 1954. Her poems have appeared in many publications, including *Blue Moon Review*, *Calyx*, *Green Mountains Review*, *Primavera*, and the anthology, *Family*. Her first poetry collection, *Vendettas, Charms, and Prayers*, won a 1997 Minnesota Voices Project Award. She teaches at the University of Wisconsin Oshkosh.

KATE GLEASON was born in New Hampshire in 1956. She is the author of two collections of poetry: *Making As If to Sing* and *The Brighter the Deeper*. Her work has appeared in such places as *Best American Poetry*, the *Los Angeles Times Book Review*, and *Green Mountains Review*, and has been anthologized in *Claiming the Spirit Within*. She teaches creative writing workshops in New Hampshire.

PAULA GOLDMAN was born in Atlantic City in 1945. Her work has appeared in such places as *North American Review*, *Harvard Review*, and *Kansas Quarterly*, and in several anthologies. She won first prize in the 1998 Louisiana Literature Prize for poetry and the 1997 *Inkwell* competition. She lives in Milwaukee.

JOY HARJO was born in 1951 in Tulsa, Oklahoma, and grew up there and in New Mexico. She attended the Institute for American Indian Arts in Santa Fe, where she later taught, and graduated from the University of New Mexico, later receiving an M.F.A. from the University of Iowa. She is the author of four collections of poetry: *What Moon Drove Me to This?*, *She Had Some Horses*, *In Mad Love and War*, and *The Woman Who Fell from the Sky*. Her latest book is *Reinventing the Enemy's Language: Contemporary Women's Writings of North America*. Harjo has received an Academy of American Poetry Award, a William Carlos Williams Award from the Poetry Society of America, a National Endowment for the Arts creative writing fellowship, among many other prestigious awards. An English professor, editor, screenwriter, and saxophone player with her band, Poetic Justice, she lives in Tucson.

DONNA HILBERT was born in Grandfield, Oklahoma, in 1946. She is the author of a poetry collection, *Deep Red*, and a collection of short stories, *Women Who Make Money and the Men Who Love Them*, which won the STAPLE First Edition Biennial Award and was published in England in 1994.

LORI HORVITZ was born in Decatur, Illinois, in 1961. Her poetry, essays, and short stories have appeared in many literary journals and anthologies, including *13th Moon*, *California Quarterly*, *Brooklyn Review*, and *The Little Magazine*. She recently completed her Ph.D. in English at SUNY at Albany.

JUDITH HOUGEN was born in Alaska and raised in the Midwest. She received an M.F.A. in creative writing from the University of Montana in 1987 and is a past recipient of the Loft-McKnight Award. Her first collection of poetry, *The Second Thing I Remember*, was a Minnesota Voices Project winner and was published in 1993. She lives in Minneapolis and teaches at Northwestern College in St. Paul.

MARIE HOWE's poems have appeared in a variety of literary magazines, including the *Atlantic*, the *New Yorker*, and *Harvard Review*. She has received fellowships from the National Endowment for the Arts and the Bunting Institute; her first book, *The Good Thief*, was selected by Margaret Atwood for the National Poetry Series. She is also the author of *What the Living Do* and coeditor of *In the Company of My Solitude: American Writing from the AIDS Pandemic*. She teaches at Sarah Lawrence College and New York University and lives in New York City.

HOLLY IGLESIAS was born in St. Louis in 1949. She is coeditor with Catherine Reid of *Every Woman I've Ever Loved: Lesbian Writers on Their Mothers* and is currently working on a family poem series, *Hankering*, and a memoir, *Breaking Down the Dam*.

ANGELA JACKSON was born in Greenville, Mississippi, raised on Chicago's South Side, and educated at Northwestern University and the University of Chicago. Her poetry collections include *And All These Roads Be Luminous: Poems Selected and New* and *Dark Legs and Silk Kisses: The Beatitudes of the Spinners*, which won the 1993 *Chicago Sun-Times* book of the year award in poetry and the 1994 Carl Sandburg Award for poetry.

HARRIET JACOBS was born in Los Angeles in 1951. Her poems have appeared in several different journals and have been anthologized in *Spirit and Flame: An Anthology of Contemporary African American Poetry*. She works as a sales executive in the financial services industry.

DIANE JARVENPA was born in St. Paul, Minnesota, in 1959. Her book of poetry, *Divining the Landscape*, was a 1994 Minnesota Voices Project winner. She is also a singer/songwriter who records under the name of Diane Jarvi. She lives in Minneapolis.

ALLISON JOSEPH is the author of

What Keeps Us Here and *Soul Train*. Her most recent collection is *In Every Seam*. She teaches at Southern Illinois University.

JULIA KASDORF grew up in western Pennsylvania and has an M.A. in creative writing and a Ph.D. in English education from New York University. Her collection entitled *Sleeping Preacher* won the Agnes Lynch Starrett Poetry Prize and was awarded the 1993 Great Lakes Colleges Association Award for new writing. Her poems have also appeared in such publications as *Poetry* and the *New Yorker*. Her latest book of poetry is *Eve's Striptease*. She teaches at Messiah College and lives in Pennsylvania.

LAURA KASISCHKE was born in Lake Charles, Louisiana, in 1961. She is the author of three books of poems: *Wild Brides*, *Housekeeping in a Dream*, and *Fire & Flower*, winner of the Beatrice Hawley Award. She has also written two novels, *Suspicious River* and *White Bird in a Blizzard*. She lives in Michigan.

JOSIE KEARNS was born in 1954. She is the author of three books of poetry: *Life after the Line*; a poetry chapbook, *New Numbers*; and a full-length collection of the same title. She received an M.F.A. from the University of Michigan in Ann Arbor, where she won three Hopwood awards, and where she now teaches writing and literature.

JULIE KING was born in Milwaukee in 1960. Her poems and short stories have been published in a wide variety of literary journals, including *Puerto del Sol*, *Gulf Coast*, and *Wisconsin Fiction*. She is also a screenwriter and filmmaker whose debut film, *Worlds*, is in now the editing process. The recipient of a grant from the Wisconsin Arts Board, she teaches writing and literature at the University of Wisconsin–Parkside.

JENNIFER LAGIER was born in Oakdale, California, in 1949. Her work has appeared in numerous journals and anthologies. She serves on the steering committee of the National Writers Union Local 7 and teaches at Hartnell College.

BARBARA LAU was born in 1951. Her poems have appeared in *Karamu*, *Southern Poetry Review*, *Iowa Woman*, *College English*, and *Borderlands*. A native Texan, she currently teaches college in the Cedar Rapids, Iowa, area and is completing an M.F.A. from Warren Wilson College.

DORIANNE LAUX was born in Augusta, Maine, in 1952. Her first book of poems, *Awake*, was nominated for the San Francisco Bay Area Book Critics award for poetry. She is also the author of *What We Carry*, a finalist for the National Book Critics Circle award for poetry. Her poems have appeared in numerous journals and anthologies, and she has received fellowships from the MacDowell Colony and the National Endowment for the Arts. With Kim Addonizio, she has also coauthored *The Poet's Companion: A Guide to the Pleasures of Writing Poetry*. She teaches at the University of Oregon in Eugene.

HARRIET LEVIN, winner of the 1996 Barnard New Women Poet's Prize for her book, *The Christmas Show*, received an M.F.A. from the University of Iowa Writers' Workshop. Her poems have appeared in a variety of literary journals, including *Partisan Review*, *New Letters*, *Iowa Review*, and *Nimrod*. She has also won the Alice Fay diCastagnola Award and the Grolier Poetry Prize. She teaches poetry to engineering students at Drexel University.

LYN LIFSHIN was born in 1949. Her latest books of poetry are *Cold Comfort* and *Bruised Velvet*. She has also edited four anthologies of women's poetry, including *Tangled Vines* and *Ariadne's Thread*, and is the subject of a documentary film, *Lyn Lifshin: Not Made of Glass*.

RACHEL LODEN was born in 1948 in Washington, D.C. Her poems have appeared in *Antioch Review*, *Boulevard*, *Chelsea*, *Paris Review*, and *New American Writing*, and have also been included in *Best American Poetry* and other anthologies. Her book, *The Last Campaign*, won the 1998 Hudson Valley Writers' Center poetry chapbook contest. She lives in Palo Alto, California.

KATHY MANGAN was born in Pittsburgh in 1950 and grew up there and in New England. She received degrees from Denison University and Ohio University, and since 1977 she has taught literature and writing at Western Maryland College, where she is a professor of English. Her poems have appeared in a number of journals, including *Georgia Review*, *Gettysburg Review*, *Shenandoah*, and *Southern Review*. Her first full-length collection of poems, *Above the Tree Line*, was published in 1995.

DONNA MASINI, a lifelong New Yorker, is a graduate of Hunter College and NYU. She has won numerous awards for her writing, including a National Endowment for the Arts poetry fellowship and a New York Foundation for the Arts award, and her poems have appeared in *Paris Review*, *Georgia Review*, *Parnassus*, *Southern Poetry Review*, and many other journals. Her poetry collection, *That Kind of Danger*, won the 1993 Barnard New Women Poets' Prize. She has been a fellow in the Yaddo Writing Program for three years and has served as a judge for the Academy of American Poets College Prize and as a member of the Bronx Council for the Arts.

REBECCA MCCLANAHAN was born in Lafayette, Indiana, in 1950. She has published three books of poetry, most recently *The Intersection of X and Y*, and two books of nonfiction, including *Word Painting: Writing More Descriptively*. Her poetry has been featured in *The Best American Poetry 1998*.

LESLIE ADRIENNE MILLER was born in Medina, Ohio, in 1956. Her books include *Staying Up for Love* (1990), *Ungodliness* (1994), and *Yesterday Had a Man in It* (1998). She has received numerous awards for her poetry, including a Loft-McKnight Award, an Artist's Assistance Grant from the Minnesota State Arts Board, and a National Endowment for the Arts fellowship. She has also won the Loft-McKnight Award of Distinction, a $20,000 prize awarded by The Loft and judge Alice Fulton in 1998. Her work is included in *The Kiss of Turning Pages*, an anthology of award-winning poetry from The Loft. She teaches at the University of St. Thomas in St. Paul, Minnesota.

LAUREL MILLS was born in Farmington, Maine, in 1946. Her poems have appeared in such publications as *Calyx* and *Ms.*, and she is the author of four award-winning books of poems, including *I Sing Back* and *The Gull Is My Divining Rod*. She teaches English at the University of Wisconsin–Fox Valley.

WENDY MNOOKIN was born in New York City in 1946. Her first book, *Guenever Speaks*, is a cycle of persona poems, and another, *Envy of the Empty Vase*, is forthcoming. She teaches poetry to children in Boston-area schools.

JUDITH MONTGOMERY was born in Torrington, Connecticut, in 1945. She is the cowinner of the 49th Parallel Poetry Prize and a finalist for the 1997 Randall Jarrell Poetry Prize. She lives in Portland, Oregon, where she is working on her first book with the aid of an Oregon Literary Arts Fellowship.

KYOKO MORI was born in Kobe, Japan, in 1957. She has lived in the Midwest since 1977, earning a Ph.D. in creative writing from the University of Wisconsin, Milwaukee. Her book of poems, *Fallout*, was published in 1994. She is also the author of two novels, *Shizuko's Daughter* and *One Bird*, and the nonfiction collections *The Dream of Water* and *Polite Lies*. Mori is an associate professor of English and writer-in-residence at St. Norbert College in De Pere, Wisconsin.

RITA RANDAZZO was born in

Brooklyn, New York, in 1945. She is the author of *Feeding Herself* and two other collections of poetry. Her work has appeared in many literary journals, webzines, and anthologies.

ANNE RICHEY, a North Carolina native, was born in 1945. Her chapbook, *Good as My Word*, was published in 1996; "Blue Thread" is from *Primavera*, a Chicago-based journal of women's fiction, poetry, and art. Ms. Richey teaches in the continuing education program at NYU.

MAUREEN SEATON is the author of four books of poetry, most recently *Furious Cooking*, which won the Iowa Poetry Prize and the Lambda Award, and *Exquisite Politics*, a collaboration with poet Denise Duhamel. Her other books are *Fear of Subways*, which won the Eighth Mountain Poetry Prize, and *The Sea among the Cupboards*, which won the 1998 Capricorn Poetry Prize. She is the recipient of a National Endowment for the Arts fellowship, an Illinois Arts Council Grant, and two Pushcart prizes, and her work has appeared in *Best American Poetry 1997*, *New Republic*, *Poetry*, and elsewhere, including on the Chicago Transit Authority's buses and subways.

PAULA SERGI was born in Fond du Lac, Wisconsin, in 1952. She is a registered nurse whose poems have been published in a wide variety of journals, including *Primavera*, *Slipstream*, *Rain City Review*, and *Small Pond*. Her first collection of poetry, *Brother*, was published in 1996, and her chapbook, *Phantom Limb*, has been a finalist in competitions. She has also published short stories and essays. She lives in Wisconsin with her husband and two sons.

DIANE SEUSS-BRAKEMAN was raised in Edwardsburg and Niles, Michigan. Her first book of poems, *It Blows You Hollow*, was published in 1998. She teaches in the creative writing program at Kalamazoo College in Kalamazoo, Michigan.

BETSY SHOLL grew up in Brick Town, New Jersey, and earned degrees from Bucknell University, University of Rochester, and Vermont College. She is the author of *Appalachian Winter* and *Rooms Overhead*, and her book *The Red Line* was selected by Ronald Wallace as the winner of the 1991 Associated Writing Programs award series in poetry. Her most recent book is *Don't Explain*, which won the Felix Pollak Prize in poetry and was published by University of Wisconsin Press in 1997.

KELLY SIEVERS was born in Green Bay, Wisconsin, in 1947. In 1965 she left Wisconsin for nursing school in Rochester, Minnesota, the subject of her poem in *Boomer Girls*. Her work has also been anthologized in *Between the Heartbeats: Poetry and Prose by Nurses.*

CATHY SONG was born in Honolulu and earned a B.A. from Wellesly College and an M.A. from Boston University. Her first book of poems, *Picture Bride*, was selected by Richard Hugo as the winner of the 1982 Yale Younger Poets Award and was nominated for the National Book Critics Circle Award. In addition, she has received the Shelley Memorial Award and the Hawaii Award for Literature. She is also the author of *School Figures*. She lives in Honolulu.

KATE SONTAG was born in Los Angeles in 1952 and received her M.F.A. from the Iowa Writers' Workshop. She has won a number of poetry awards, including the Ron Bayes Poetry Prize in 1995, and her work has appeared in many journals, including *Green Mountains Review, Kalliope, Salt Hill Journal, Blue Moon Review*, and *Prairie Schooner*. She teaches composition, creative writing, and literature at the University of Wisconsin Oshkosh.

MICHELE SPRING-MOORE was born near Binghamton, New York, in 1963. Her poetry and essays have been published in various journals, including *Hanging Loose* and *Many Mountains Moving*, and has been anthologized in *Plural Desires: Writing Bisexual Women's Realities*. She earned her M.A. in poetry at the University of Colorado in Boulder and lives in Rochester, New York, where she works as a writer and political organizer.

LAURA STEARNS was born in Seattle in 1957. She has published poetry, fiction, children's stories, and personal essays. Her one-act play, *Burning Bride*, has been performed on National Public Radio. She lives in San Francisco, contracting her writing services to Bay Area corporations.

ALISON STONE was born in Framingham, Massachusetts, in 1964. Her poems have appeared in *Paris Review, Poetry, Ploughshares*, and a variety of other journals, and her book, *Persephone Returning*, has been a finalist in national competitions. She is also a painter who has exhibited her work in New York, Massachusetts, and Rhode Island. She earns her living as a psychotherapist, yoga instructor, and Reiki master in New York City.

JOYCE SUTPHEN, a native Minnesotan, won the 1994 Barnard New Women Poets Prize for her poetry collection entitled *Straight Out of View*. Her poems have appeared in such journals as *Poetry, Spoon River Poetry Review*, and *Birmingham Review*, and she has taught creative writing and English at the University of Minnesota. She lives in Minneapolis.

ALISON TOWNSEND was born in Allentown, Pennsylvania, in 1953. Her poetry, essays, and reviews have appeared in magazines such as *Prairie Schooner*, *Georgia Review*, *Calyx*, and *Women's Review of Books*, and have also been anthologized, most recently *Claiming the Spirit Within* and *The Party Train: A Collection of North American Prose Poems*. She teaches English and creative writing at the University of Wisconsin Whitewater, as well as in a private workshop for women called *In Our Own Voices*.

ANN TOWNSEND was born in Pittsburgh in 1962. She is the author of three chapbooks, and her poems, stories, and essays have appeared in the *Nation*, *Kenyon Review*, *Southern Review*, *TriQuarterly*, and many other magazines. Her first full-length collection of poetry, *Dime Store Erotics*, winner of the Gerald Cable Prize, was published in 1998. She teaches at Denison University and is the director of the Jonathan Reynolds Young Writers Workshop.

NATASHA TRETHEWEY was born in Gulfport, Mississippi, in 1966. Her poems have appeared in *American Poetry Review*, *Gettysburg Review*, *North American Review*, and *Southern Review*, and have been anthologized in *Spirit and Flame: An Anthology of Contemporary African American Poetry*. She teaches at Auburn University.

PATRICIA VALDATA was born in New Brunswick, New Jersey, in 1952 and received her M.F.A. from Goddard College in 1991. Her poems have appeared in *Onion River Review*, *Icarus*, and *Phoebe: An Interdisciplinary Journal of Feminist Scholarship*. She is also the author of a novel, *Crosswind*.

JUDITH VOLLMER was born in Wilkinsburg, Pennsylvania, in 1951. Her first book of poems, *Level Green*, won the Brittingham Prize in 1990, and her newest collection, *The Door Open to the Fire*, won the Cleveland State Poetry Prize in 1997. She directs the writing program at the University of Pittsburgh at Greensburg.

MARY WEEMS was born in Cleveland in 1954. She is the author of *Blackeyed* and *white*, which was a Wick Chapbook selection by Kent State University Press in 1996. Her work has appeared in many magazines, including *African American Review*, *Calyx*, and *Pearl*, and has been anthologized in *Spirit and Flame: An Anthology of Contemporary African American Poetry*. She is currently a doctoral student in education policy studies at the University of Illinois.

Permissions

We are grateful to the authors who have given us permission to include previously unpublished work in this anthology. We also thank the authors, editors, and publishers who have given us permission to reprint the following selections.

KIM ADDONIZIO: "The Philosopher's Club" and "Them," copyright © 1994. Reprinted from *The Philosopher's Club* with the permission of BOA Editions, 260 East Ave., Rochester, N.Y.

ELIZABETH ALEXANDER: "Apollo," "Summertime," and "Affirmative Action Blues (1993)" from *Body of Life* (Tia Chucha Press, 1996). Copyright © 1996 by Elizabeth Alexander. Reprinted by permission of the author.

JULIA ALVAREZ: "Queens, 1963" and "The Word Made Flesh" (excerpt from "Sound Bites") from *The Other Side / El Otro Lado*. Copyright © 1995 by Julia Alvarez. Published by Plume Penguin, an imprint of Dutton, a division of Penguin USA and originally in hardcover by Dutton Signet. Reprinted by permission of Susan Bergholz Literary Services, New York.

DOROTHY BARRESI: "Vacation, 1969" from *All of the Above* by Dorothy Barresi. Copyright © 1991 by Dorothy Barresi. Reprinted by permission of Beacon Press.

JAN BEATTY: "If This Is Sex, It Must Be Tuesday" and "Mad River" from *Mad River*, by Jan Beatty, © 1995. Reprinted by permission of the University of Pittsburgh Press.

SHEILA BENDER: "With Martha at Gig Harbor" from *Sustenence: New and Selected Poems*, copyright © 1997 by Sheila Bender. Reprinted by permission of the author.

JILL BIALOSKY: "Fathers in the Snow" (excerpt) and "Stairway to Heaven" from *The End of Desire* (Knopf, 1997). Copyright © 1997 by Jill Bialosky. Reprinted by permission of Alfred A. Knopf.

MARIANNE BORUCH: "The Vietnam Birthday Lottery, 1970" from *A Stick That Breaks and Breaks*. Copyright © 1997 by Oberlin College. Reprinted by permission of Oberlin College Press.

JEANNE BRYNER: "Butterfly" from *Breathless* (Wick Poetry Chapbook Series, Kent State University Press, 1995). Copyright © 1995 by Jeanne Bryner. Reprinted by permission of the author.

MARILYN CHIN: "First Lessons" from *Dwarf Bamboo* by Marilyn Chin (Greenfield Review Press,

1987). Copyright © 1987 by Marilyn Chin. Reprinted by permission of the author.

SANDRA CISNEROS: "My Wicked Wicked Ways" from *My Wicked Wicked Ways*. Copyright © 1987 by Sandra Cisneros. Published by Third Woman Press and in hardcover by Alfred A. Knopf. Reprinted by permission of Susan Bergholz Literary Services, New York.

GERALDINE CONNOLLY: "Movie Queens" (originally published in *Connecticut Review*), copyright © 1996 by Geraldine Connolly. Reprinted by permission of the author. "An Afternoon in the World" (originally published in *Poetry Northwest*) from *Province of Fire* by Geraldine Connolly (Iris Press, 1998). Copyright © 1998 by Geraldine Connolly. Reprinted by permission of the author.

BARBARA CROOKER: "Nearing Menopause, I Run Into Elvis at Shoprite" (originally published in *Karamu*), copyright ©1996 by Barbara Crooker. Reprinted by permission of the author.

SILVIA CURBELO: "Janis Joplin" (originally published in *Calyx*) from *The Secret History of Water* (Anhinga Press, 1997). Copyright © 1997 by Silvia Curbelo. Reprinted by permission of the author and Anhinga Press.

RITA DOVE: "Adolescence—I," "Adolescence—II," "Adolescence—III" from Rita Dove, *Selected Poems* (Vintage Books, 1993). Copyright © 1980 by Rita Dove. Reprinted by permission of the author.

DENISE DUHAMEL: "Feminism" and "Ragweed" from *Girl Soldier* (Garden Street Press, 1996). Copyright © 1996 by Denise Duhamel. Reprinted by permission of the author. "On Being Born the Same Exact Day of the Same Exact Year as Boy George" from *Smile!* (Warm Spring Press, 1993). Copyright © 1993 by Denise Duhamel. Reprinted by permission of the author.

KELLY NORMAN ELLIS: "Girl," originally published in *Spirit & Flame: An Anthology of Contemporary African American Poetry*, edited by Keith Gilyard (Syracuse University Press, 1997). Copyright © 1997 by Kelly Norman Ellis. Reprinted by permission of the author.

LYNN EMANUEL: "The Planet Krypton" from *The Dig and Hotel Fiesta*. Copyright © 1995 by Lynn Emanuel. Reprinted by permission of the author and University of Illinois Press.

HEID ERDRICH: "True Myth" and "Creation" from *Fishing for Myth* (New Rivers Press, 1997). Copyright © 1997 by Heid Erdrich. Reprinted by permission of the author.

SUSAN FIRER: "An Autobiography of An Angel" and "Basement Slow Dancing" from *The Lives of the Saints and Everything* (Cleveland State University Poetry Center, 1993). Copyright ©

1993 by Susan Firer. Reprinted by permission of the author and Cleveland State University Poetry Center.

PAMELA GEMIN: "When Van Morrison Sang" (originally published in *Green Mountains Review*) and "Senior Picture, 1971" (originally published in *Blue Moon Review*) from *Vendettas, Charms and Prayers* (New Rivers Press, 1999). Copyright © 1999 by Pamela Gemin. Reprinted by permission of the author.

KATE GLEASON: "The Age of Unlimited Possibilities" and "In Winter Something inside Me Returns as to a Dark God" from *The Brighter the Deeper* (Embers, 1995). Copyright © 1995 by Kate Gleason. Reprinted by permission of the author.

JOY HARJO: "Rainy Dawn" and "Crystal Lake" from *In Mad Love & War* (Wesleyan University Press, 1990). Copyright © 1990 by Joy Harjo. Reprinted by permission of the University Press of New England.

DONNA HILBERT: "Craving" and "The Pursuit of Knowledge" (originally published in *Pearl*) from *Feathers and Dust* (Event Horizon Press, 1996). Copyright © 1996 by Donna Hilbert. Reprinted by permission of the author.

JUDITH HOUGEN: "Coming of Age," "Fitness Club: Riding the Lifecycle," and "Points of No Return" from *The Second Thing I Remember* (New Rivers Press, 1993). Copyright © 1993 by Judith Hougen. Reprinted by permission of the author.

MARIE HOWE: "The Boy" from *What the Living Do* by Marie Howe. Copyright © 1997 by Marie Howe. Reprinted by permission of W. W. Norton & Company.

ANGELA JACKSON: "Blue Milk" and "Faith" from *And All These Roads Be Luminous: Poems Selected and New* by Angela Jackson (TriQuarterly Books/Northwestern University Press, 1998). Copyright © 1998 by Angela Jackson. Reprinted by permission of TriQuarterly Books/Northwestern University Press.

HARRIET JACOBS: "growing into my name," originally published in *Spirit and Flame: An Anthology of Contemporary African American Poetry*, edited by Keith Gilyard (Syracuse University Press, 1997). Copyright © 1997 by Harriet Jacobs. Reprinted by permission of the author.

DIANE JARVENPA: "The Other Language" from *Divining the Landscape* (New Rivers Press, 1996). Copyright © 1997 by Diane Jarvenpa. Reprinted by permission of the author.

ALLISON JOSEPH: "The First Time," "Traitor," and "Screen Test" from *In Every Seam*, by Allison Joseph, copyright © 1997. Reprinted by permission of the University of Pittsburgh Press.

JULIA KASDORF: "First TV in a Mennonite Family," "Catholics," and "After the Second Miscarriage" from *Sleeping Preacher*, by Julia Kasdorf, copyright © 1992. Reprinted by permission of the University of Pittsburgh Press.

LAURA KASISCHKE: "Fatima" from *Housekeeping in a Dream* by Laura Kasischke (Carnegie Mellon University Press, 1995). Copyright © 1995 by Laura Kasischke. Reprinted by permission of the author.

JULIE KING: "To Mary at Thirteen" (originally appeared in *Cottonwood*), copyright © 1995 by Julie King. Reprinted by permission of the author.

DORIANNE LAUX: "Small Gods," "Fast Gas," and "Twelve" from *What We Carry*. Copyright © 1994 by Dorianne Laux. Reprinted by permission of BOA Editions, 260 East Ave., Rochester, N.Y.

HARRIET LEVIN: "Bird of Paradise" and "The Christmas Show" from *The Christmas Show* by Harriet Levin. Copyright © 1997 by Harriet Levin. Reprinted by permission of Beacon Press, Boston.

LYN LIFSHIN: "elaine" from *Cold Comfort* (Black Sparrow Press, 1997). Copyright © 1997 by Lyn Lifshin. Reprinted by permission of the author.

RACHEL LODEN: "Marrying the Stranger" (originally published in *Yellow Silk*), copyright © 1990 by Rachel Loden. Reprinted by permission of the author.

KATHY MANGAN: "St. Paul Street Seasonal" from *Above the Tree Line*. Copyright © 1995 by Kathy Mangan. Reprinted by permission of Carnegie Mellon University Press.

DONNA MASINI: "Claim," "Getting Out of Where We Came From," and "My Mother Makes Me a Geisha Girl" from *That Kind of Danger* by Donna Masini. Copyright © 1994 by Donna Masini. Reprinted by permission of Beacon Press, Boston.

REBECCA McCLANAHAN: "Bridal Rites" from *Mother Tongue* (University of Central Florida Press, 1982). Copyright © 1982 by Rebecca McClanahan. Reprinted by permission of the author. "Passion Week, 1966" (originally published in *Southern Poetry Review*), copyright © 1997 by Rebecca McClanahan. Reprinted by permission of the author.

LESLIE ADRIENNE MILLER: "Lawn Ornaments" (originally published in *Crab Orchard Review*) and "Warts" (originally published in *River Styx*) from *Yesterday Had a Man in It* (Carnegie Mellon University Press, 1998). Copyright © 1998 by Leslie Adrienne Miller. Reprinted by permission of the author. "Sleeping Out" (originally published in *Nimrod*), from *Ungodliness* (Carnegie Mellon University Press, 1994). Copyright © 1994 by Leslie Adrienne Miller. Reprinted by permission of the author.

LAUREL MILLS: "Learning Our Names" (originally published in *Common Lives, Lesbian Lives*), from *I Sing Back* (Black Hat Press, 1998). Copyright © 1998 by Laurel Mills. Reprinted by permission of the author.

JUDITH MONTGOMERY: "Taking the Fences" excerpt from "A Natural History of Fences" (originally published in *convolvulus*), copyright © 1998 by Judith Montgomery. Reprinted by permission of the author.

WENDY MNOOKIN: "Polio Summer" (originally published in *Poetpourri*), copyright © 1990 by Wendy Mnookin. Reprinted by permission of the author.

KYOKO MORI: "Barbie Says Math Is Hard" and "On the Edge of the Field" from *Fallout* (Tia Chucha Press, 1994). Copyright © 1994 by Kyoko Mori. Reprinted by permission of the author.

ANNE RICHEY: "Blue Thread" (originally published in *Primavera*), from *Good as My Word*. Copyright © 1996 by Anne Richey. Reprinted by permission of the author.

MAUREEN SEATON: "Mortal Sins" and "The Contract / 1968" from *The Sea among the Cupboards* (New Rivers Press, 1992). Copyright © 1992 by Maureen Seaton. Reprinted by permission of the author.

DIANE SEUSS-BRAKEMAN: "What Is There" and "Let Go" (originally published in *Primavera*), copyright © 1995 by Diane Seuss-Brakeman. Reprinted by permission of the author.

BETSY SHOLL: "Sex Ed" from *The Red Line*, by Betsy Sholl, copyright © 1992. Reprinted by permission of the University of Pittsburgh Press.

KELLY SIEVERS: "Rochester, Minnesota, 1965" (originally published in *The Bridge* and later in *Western Journal of Medicine* and *Between the Heartbeats: Prose and Poetry by Nurses*, edited by Cortney Davis and Judy Schaefer, University of Iowa Press, 1995), copyright © 1993 by Kelly Sievers. Reprinted by permission of the author.

CATHY SONG: "The Grammar of Silk," "Eat," and "Sunworshippers" from *School Figures*, by Cathy Song, copyright © 1994. Reprinted by permission of the University of Pittsburgh Press.

MICHELE SPRING-MOORE: "Adolescent Rag: Greece, New York, 1981" (originally published in *Hanging Loose*), copyright © 1994 by Michele Spring-Moore. Reprinted by permission of the author.

LAURA STEARNS: "Barn Swallows" (originally published in *Seattle*

Review), copyright © 1993 by Laura Stearns. Reprinted by permission of the author.

ALISON STONE: "Rocket to Russia" (originally published in *Poetry*), copyright © 1987 by The Modern Poetry Association. Reprinted by permission of the Editor of *Poetry*.

JOYCE SUTPHEN: "Crossroads," from *Straight Out of View*. Copyright © 1995 by Joyce Sutphen. Reprinted by permission of Beacon Press, Boston.

ANN TOWNSEND: "Institutional Blue" from *Dime Store Erotics* (Silverfish Review Press, 1998). Copyright © 1998 by Ann Townsend. Reprinted by permission of Silverfish Review Press.

NATASHA TRETHEWEY: "Collection Day" (originally published in *Massachusetts Review* and later in *Spirit and Flame: An Anthology of Contemporary African American Poetry*, edited by Keith Gilyard, Syracuse University Press, 1997), copyright © 1996 by Natasha Trethewey. Reprinted by permission of the author.

JUDITH VOLLMER: "Wildsisters Bar" from *Level Green* (University of Wisconsin Press, 1990). Copyright © 1990 by Judith Vollmer. Reprinted by permission of the author.

MARY WEEMS: "Return to Temptation" (originally published in *Spirit and Flame: An Anthology of Contemporary African American Poetry*, edited by Keith Gilyard, Syracuse University Press, 1997) from *White* (Wick Chapbook Series, Kent State University Press, 1997). Copyright © 1997 by Mary Weems. Reprinted by permission of the author.

Index